Weight Loss and Stress Eating

The Cortisol Trap

Understanding Cortisol, Cravings, and Why Diets Alone Don't Fix It

Naomi Everhart

First edition, 2026

Published by Naomi Everhart

This book is intended for general educational and reflective purposes only. It is not a substitute for professional financial, legal, medical, or mental health advice, diagnosis, or treatment. Always seek the advice of a qualified professional with any questions regarding your specific circumstances. Never disregard professional advice or delay seeking it because of something you have read in this book. Names and identifying details in any illustrative examples are anonymous/archetypal composites, not depictions of a single real individual.

Contents

Chapter 1: Chapter 1: The Stress Signal

The chipped Formica countertop felt cold under my forearm. Not uncomfortably so, just…present. A grounding sensation in a day that had been anything but. I was staring at a half-eaten plate of diner fries, lukewarm and dusted with enough salt to register on the Richter scale. It wasn't hunger driving me here, not exactly. It was more like an insistent static beneath my skin, a low-humming anxiety that always seemed to find its way back to this booth at 11:47 PM on a Tuesday.

My body was screaming at me. Had been for hours. I just hadn't wanted to listen.

Across from me, the waitress—Darlene, I think her name was—refilled my water glass without a word. She'd seen me enough times over the last few months to know the drill. The late-night arrival, the order of fries (always fries), the vacant stare aimed somewhere beyond the flickering fluorescent lights. She wasn't judging. Darlene had *seen* things. This diner was a repository of quiet desperation, a place where people came not for nourishment but for temporary reprieve from whatever their lives had become.

That's the thing about stress signals. They don't arrive with klaxons and flashing lights. They whisper. A tightness in your jaw you don't notice until you're grinding your teeth at a stoplight. A craving for salt and grease that feels like need, not choice. The way you snap at someone you love over something trivial, then hate yourself for it later. These aren't character flaws. They're messages. Your body, in its ancient wisdom, trying desperately to tell you something's wrong.

And we've gotten terrifyingly good at ignoring them.

Think about it. When's the last time you felt genuinely relaxed? Not distracted—scrolling through social media doesn't count—but actually at ease in your own skin? For most of us, it's been so long we've forgotten what it feels like. We've normalized a constant state of low-grade panic, mistaking it for productivity, for being needed, for mattering.

Here's what I wish someone had told me twenty years ago: cortisol doesn't care about your ambitions. It doesn't distinguish between a genuine emergency and a difficult email from your boss. It floods your system either way, preparing you for a threat that almost never requires the response it's triggering. Your heart rate spikes. Your muscles tense. Glucose dumps into your bloodstream. Your digestive system shuts down—who needs to process food when you're supposedly fighting for your life?

Except you're not fighting for your life. You're sitting in a meeting. Or stuck in traffic. Or lying awake at three in the morning replaying a conversation from two days ago, convinced you said the wrong thing.

The physiological response remains the same regardless. And that's where everything starts to break down.

I'm not some detached observer here, by the way. I'm writing this at 6:23 AM after sleeping maybe four hours, fueled by coffee that's too strong and the vague anxiety that I haven't adequately captured what I'm trying to say. My shoulders are up around my ears. I've checked my email twice since starting this paragraph. The irony isn't lost on me. I teach this stuff, and I still fall into the trap. That's how insidious it is.

Let me tell you about Amelia Earhart. Not the mythologized icon, fearless and untouchable, but the woman behind the goggles. In the weeks leading up to her final flight in 1937, she was exhausted. Bone-deep, can't-think-straight exhausted. The logistics alone were crushing—coordinating with sponsors, managing a crew, dealing with mechanical setbacks, facing relentless public scrutiny. Every decision mattered. Every delay felt catastrophic.

Her body would have been awash in cortisol. The same hormone that helped our ancestors outrun predators was flooding her system in response to pressure that was real, yes, but not the kind you can physically escape. She couldn't run from deadlines. Couldn't fight off skepticism. The only option was to push through. And she did. Until she disappeared somewhere over the Pacific, her final radio transmissions increasingly frantic, disoriented.

I'm not saying stress killed Amelia Earhart. Navigation challenges and limited fuel did that. But chronic exhaustion clouds judgment. Makes you miss things. Erodes the very faculties you need most when everything's on the line.

We like to believe we're different. That we can operate at peak performance indefinitely if we just optimize hard enough—sleep hack our way to resilience, biohack our stress response, productivity-hack our way out of overwhelm. But you can't hack biology. You can only ignore it for so long before it stops sending polite signals and starts taking more drastic measures.

I learned this the hard way. November, four years ago. My first book was about to launch, and I'd convinced myself that everything hinged on it. Not just the book's success, but my entire sense of worth as a writer, as a human being. Every minor setback felt apocalyptic. A delayed cover proof. A lukewarm advance review. An interview that didn't land the way I'd hoped.

I stopped sleeping properly. Started eating erratically—sometimes forgetting meals entirely, other times standing at the kitchen counter at midnight shoveling down whatever required the least preparation. Crackers. Cheese. Cold pizza. It wasn't about hunger. It was about filling a void that had nothing to do with food.

My wife found me one night around 2 AM, meticulously reorganizing the spice rack while simultaneously answering emails on my phone. She didn't say anything about the book, or deadlines, or any of the things I was ostensibly stressed about. Just stood there for a moment, watching me alphabetize cumin and coriander, then asked quietly, "Did you eat dinner?"

I hadn't. The idea of taking thirty minutes to sit down and eat felt impossibly indulgent. I had too much to do. Too much riding on getting everything perfect.

"You're going to make yourself sick," she said. Not angry. Just sad.

She was right. Within a week, I came down with the worst flu I'd had in a decade. My body, tired of sending subtle signals I refused to acknowledge, simply shut me down. Forced me into stillness the only way it could.

That's cortisol's endgame when you ignore it long enough. The signal gets louder. More insistent. More destructive.

Here's what's happening physiologically. When you encounter a stressor—let's say a tight deadline—your hypothalamus (a tiny region at the base of your brain) activates your sympathetic nervous system. This triggers your adrenal glands to release adrenaline, which makes your heart pound and your breathing quicken. Then comes cortisol, the hormone that maintains this heightened state, keeping you alert and energized.

In short bursts, this is magnificent. Cortisol is why our ancestors survived. It sharpens focus. Boosts energy. Dampens pain. If you're being chased by something with teeth, you *want* this response.

But when the stressor doesn't go away—when your inbox never empties, when your to-do list keeps growing, when financial pressure or relationship tension becomes the water you swim in—cortisol stays elevated. And prolonged cortisol exposure is toxic.

It suppresses your immune system, making you more susceptible to everything from colds to chronic illness. It interferes with memory and learning. It contributes to anxiety and depression. It disrupts your sleep-wake cycle, leaving you wired and exhausted simultaneously. And—this is the kicker—it intensifies your cravings for high-calorie, high-fat, high-sugar foods.

Because your body, still operating under the assumption that you're facing physical danger, wants quick energy. It doesn't want a kale salad. It wants something dense, immediately metabolizable. Something that tastes like survival.

That's why I was eating cold fries in a diner at midnight. Not because I lacked discipline. Not because I was weak. But because my body was begging for relief from a threat that didn't exist in any form I could physically combat.

Dr. Maya Angelou understood this, I think. I interviewed her once, years ago, shortly before her eightieth birthday. She was radiant. Not in the Instagram-filter way, but genuinely alive, present, engaged. I asked her how she maintained that kind of equanimity given everything she'd survived—the trauma of her childhood, decades of systemic racism and sexism, the constant demand to perform her wisdom for an audience that didn't always deserve it.

She didn't talk about meditation apps or morning routines. She talked about her garden.

"Getting my hands in the dirt," she said, smiling in a way that made you feel seen, "reminds me I'm part of something bigger than myself. That even in chaos, things grow. Things heal."

It wasn't about *escaping* stress. It was about grounding herself in something tangible, something restorative. She wasn't trying to eliminate cortisol—that's impossible, and undesirable—but to counterbalance it with experiences that signaled safety. That told her nervous system: you're okay. You can rest.

We've lost that. We've built a culture that glorifies busyness, that treats exhaustion as a credential. We brag about how little we sleep. How much we juggle. How indispensable we are. And we've started believing that self-care—actual, unglamorous care for our basic needs—is selfish. Weak. Something you do only after you've earned it by burning yourself out.

But here's the truth: you can't earn the right to be human. You already are one. And human bodies require things. Sleep. Nourishment. Movement. Connection. Stillness. These aren't luxuries. They're prerequisites for functioning.

I think about Sarah Chen a lot. She was a corporate lawyer I worked with two years ago—brilliant, meticulous, drowning. Her days were a relentless grind of billable hours, client demands, and court appearances. She barely slept. Lived on coffee and takeout. Her marriage was fraying. She couldn't remember the last time she'd laughed.

Every evening, she'd find herself on food delivery apps, scrolling mindlessly, ordering things she didn't even want. Thai food one night. Pizza the next. It wasn't about enjoyment. It was about numbing. A brief respite from the pressure crushing her from all sides.

She knew it wasn't healthy. That knowledge made it worse. She'd eat, feel guilty, stress about the guilt, and order more food the next night. Classic cortisol trap: stress triggers craving, craving leads to behavior that temporarily soothes but ultimately amplifies the stress, creating a self-perpetuating loop.

When we first talked, Sarah kept apologizing. For taking up my time. For being "dramatic." For not having her life together despite being objectively successful by every external measure.

"I just need to be stronger," she said.

No. She needed to be *kinder*. To herself. To the body that was doing its absolute best to keep her alive despite the impossible demands she was placing on it.

The signal Sarah's body was sending—the exhaustion, the cravings, the emotional numbness—wasn't a failure. It was *information*. Her nervous system, in its infinite wisdom, was screaming that something had to change. That she couldn't sustain this pace. That the threat she was responding to wasn't a predator she could outrun, but a lifestyle that was slowly killing her.

You might be thinking: easy for me to say. That I'm sitting here pontificating about stress management while conveniently admitting my own struggles with late-night fries and 2 AM spice-rack reorganization. And you'd be right to call that out. I am imperfect. I backslide constantly. That's precisely why I'm writing this—not from some mountaintop of enlightenment, but from the arena, covered in the same dirt you are.

The difference, maybe, is that I've learned to recognize the signal earlier now. Not always. Not perfectly. But more often than I used to.

That tightness in my chest? That's not ambition. It's anxiety.

The urge to keep working past the point of diminishing returns? That's not dedication. It's avoidance.

The craving for something—anything—to take the edge off? That's my body telling me I've been running on cortisol fumes for too long and it needs actual rest, not a distraction.

Learning to read these signals is the work. Not eliminating them. Not transcending them. Just…noticing. And then, when you're ready, responding with something other than judgment or numbing.

Here's what that might look like in practice.

Tonight, before you reach for your phone or turn on the TV or pour that third glass of wine, pause. Literally stop moving for sixty seconds. Close your eyes if that feels comfortable. Otherwise, just let your gaze soften, unfocused.

Notice your breathing. You don't have to change it. Just observe. Is it shallow? Rapid? Held?

Notice your body. Where are you holding tension? Your jaw? Your shoulders? Your stomach?

Notice what you're feeling. Not what you *should* feel, or what you wish you felt, but what's actually present. Anxiety? Exhaustion? Restlessness? Numbness?

Don't try to fix any of it. Don't layer on self-improvement. Don't turn this into another task you can fail at. Just notice. For sixty seconds. That's it.

This isn't meditation. It's not mindfulness in any formal sense. It's reconnaissance. You're gathering intel about your own nervous system. Learning to read the signals before they escalate into something that forces you to pay attention—a panic attack, a breakdown, a flu that knocks you flat for a week.

Because here's the thing about cortisol: it's not your enemy. It's a messenger. And like any messenger, it gets louder when you ignore it. Those whispers—the tight jaw, the craving, the irritability—those are the gentle warnings. If you keep ignoring them, the message escalates. Insomnia. Digestive issues. Chronic pain. Depression. Burnout so complete you can barely get out of bed.

Your body doesn't want to hurt you. It wants to protect you. But protection requires your cooperation. It requires that you actually *listen* when it tells you something's wrong.

I wish I could tell you there's a hack for this. A five-step process that fixes everything. But the truth is messier. It's sixty seconds here. A moment of awareness there. Small choices, repeated over time, that gradually shift your relationship with your own nervous system.

It's choosing to eat lunch sitting down instead of at your desk.

It's taking three deep breaths before responding to an email that makes your blood pressure spike.

It's going to bed at a reasonable hour even when there's more work to do.

It's saying no to something you don't have capacity for, even when you're afraid of disappointing someone.

It's recognizing that the fries, the ice cream, the mindless scrolling—those aren't the problem. They're the symptom. And shaming yourself for the symptom just adds more stress to an already overloaded system.

What would it feel like to treat yourself the way you'd treat someone you loved who was struggling? Not with pity, but with compassion. With the understanding that they're doing their best in impossible circumstances, and that what they need most isn't judgment but kindness.

Because that's what we're talking about here. Not willpower. Not discipline. Not optimization. Just basic human kindness directed inward. The revolutionary act of listening to your body's signals and believing they matter. That *you* matter. Not because of what you produce or achieve, but simply because you exist.

The cortisol will keep coming. Stress is part of life. But how you respond to that signal—whether you treat it as an enemy to suppress or information to act on—that's where your power lives.

And in the next chapter, we're going to talk about one of the most overlooked sources of cortisol dysregulation: the profound human need for connection, and what happens when we try to carry our stress alone. Because it turns out the antidote to chronic stress isn't willpower or productivity hacks. It's something far older, far simpler, and far more threatening to the armor most of us have built around our vulnerability.

What would happen if you stopped trying to outrun the signal? If you turned toward it instead, curious about what it might be trying to tell you?

Darlene refilled my coffee without asking, and I caught the look she gave the untouched fries—not judgment exactly, more like recognition.

Darlene refilled my coffee without asking, and I caught the look she gave the untouched fries—not judgment exactly, more like recognition. Once your body reads everything as a threat, it starts demanding specific solutions, and the first solution it screams for is immediate relief.

Chapter 2: Chapter 2: Craving Connections

When was the last time you ate something you didn't actually want? Not that you didn't enjoy it—that's different—but that you reached for it while your conscious mind was occupied with something else entirely, and only afterward realized your hand had moved on its own?

This is the part where I'm supposed to tell you I've conquered this pattern entirely, that I've transcended the cortisol-dopamine loop through sheer mindfulness and green smoothies. I haven't. What I *have* done is gotten better at catching myself mid-almond, recognizing the circuit that's running, and—sometimes, not always—choosing something else. But the pull is still there. It probably always will be.

The reason I'm telling you this isn't to normalize stress eating or let either of us off the hook. It's because the first step in breaking any cycle is admitting you're in one, and the second is understanding why your brain keeps looping the same track. The chocolate bar you reached for after that brutal meeting yesterday wasn't a failure of willpower. It was your brain doing exactly what evolution wired it to do: seek reward when threat levels spike. The problem is, your brain's reward system was designed for a world where "threat" meant a predator in the bushes, not an email from your boss with the subject line "Quick question about your report."

Let's talk about what's actually happening in your skull when stress sends you hunting through the pantry.

When cortisol floods your system—whether from a looming deadline, a fight with your partner, or a passive-aggressive Slack message—it doesn't just make you feel anxious. It recalibrates your brain's reward circuitry, making you hypersensitive to anything that promises a quick dopamine hit. And few things deliver dopamine faster than sugar and fat. That's not a character flaw. That's neurochemistry.

Dopamine is the brain's currency of motivation and pleasure. It's what surges when you bite into something sweet, when you get a text from someone you're excited to hear from, when you cross the finish line of a hard run. It's the neurotransmitter that says, *Yes, this—more of this.* Under normal circumstances, your brain regulates dopamine release with a fairly steady hand. But when cortisol spikes, that regulation goes out the window. Suddenly, your brain is a desperate investor throwing money at any asset that might pay out immediately.

The classic example here is the study out of UCSF in the early 2000s—not the one you're thinking of, but close—that looked at how chronic stress reshapes eating behavior in women. Researchers found that women under sustained stress consistently gravitated toward high-calorie, high-sugar foods, and the effect was strongest in those with elevated cortisol. The mechanism wasn't mysterious: stress hormones were literally rewriting their food preferences in real time, tilting the scale toward anything that could deliver a fast reward.

Here's the part that makes this so hard to break: the relief is *real.* That cookie, that slice of pizza, that handful of chips—they genuinely do make you feel better. For ten minutes. Maybe twenty. Dopamine floods in, cortisol dips, and your nervous system exhales. The problem is, the stress that triggered the craving is still there. The deadline didn't move. The argument didn't resolve. And now, on top of the original stressor, you've got a new layer of guilt and frustration because you "gave in" again.

So you're back where you started, only now you feel worse. And guess what your brain suggests as a solution? More dopamine. More reward. Another trip to the kitchen.

This is the loop. Stress triggers cortisol. Cortisol sensitizes you to dopamine. Dopamine-rich foods provide temporary relief. Relief fades. Stress remains. Repeat.

You might be thinking, *Okay, but I know this already. I know I'm stress eating. Knowing doesn't stop me from doing it.* And you're right. Awareness alone isn't enough. If it were, every smoker who ever read the surgeon general's warning would have quit on the spot. The gap between understanding a pattern and changing it is where most people get stuck, and it's where mindfulness actually starts to matter—not as some vague Instagram-wellness concept, but as a specific, practical tool for interrupting the circuit before it completes.

Mindfulness, in this context, means one thing: putting space between the trigger and your response. That's it. Not achieving zen. Not clearing your mind of all thoughts. Just noticing the urge *before* you're halfway through the bag of chips, and choosing—consciously, deliberately—what happens next.

Let me give you a concrete example, because abstract advice is useless.

It's Thursday evening. You've been in back-to-back meetings since 9 a.m., you skipped lunch, and you just got an email that a project you thought was done needs to be completely reworked by Monday. Your stress level is a seven out of ten and climbing. You walk into your kitchen, open the fridge, and stand there scanning for something—anything—that will make the tightness in your chest ease up.

Here's where mindfulness comes in. Instead of grabbing whatever looks good and eating it over the sink while you stare at your phone, you pause. Just for ten seconds. You take three deep breaths—slow inhale through your nose, longer exhale through your mouth. You don't try to talk yourself out of eating. You just notice what's happening in your body. Tight shoulders. Shallow breathing. A low-level hum of panic in your gut.

And then you ask yourself one question: *Am I actually hungry, or am I trying to feel less terrible?*

If the answer is hunger, eat. If the answer is anything else—stress, loneliness, frustration, exhaustion—then food isn't the solution. It's a temporary patch on a wound that needs something else entirely.

This is not a magic trick. The first fifty times you try this, you'll probably still eat the thing. But what you're doing, slowly, is training your brain to recognize the pattern *while it's happening* instead of twenty minutes later when the bag is empty and you're annoyed at yourself. That recognition—that tiny sliver of space between stimulus and response—is where change actually lives.

I started doing this about two years ago, and I'm still not great at it. There are weeks where I catch myself every time, where I choose the walk around the block instead of the drawer of dark chocolate. And there are weeks where I'm three cookies deep before I even remember I was supposed to be paying attention. The difference now is that I don't treat the latter as failure. I treat it as data. *What was I feeling right before I reached for that? What did I need that I wasn't getting?*

Usually, it's one of two things: I'm either trying to numb something uncomfortable, or I'm trying to fill a void that food can't actually fill. The second one—the loneliness piece—is harder to admit, but it's more common than most of us want to acknowledge.

We don't talk enough about how much of our eating is driven not by hunger or even stress, but by a lack of connection. You come home to an empty apartment after a long day, and the silence is too loud, so you turn on the TV and eat dinner standing up in front of the fridge. Not because you're ravenous. Because sitting down alone at a table feels too stark, too much like an admission that no one's there.

Food is warm. Food is reliable. Food doesn't cancel plans or forget to text back. And when your brain is starved for connection—real, human, face-to-face connection—it'll take the substitute reward of a bowl of pasta or a pint of ice cream, because at least that's *something*.

This is where the chapter title comes from. Craving Connections. Because half the time, what we're reaching for isn't actually food. It's the feeling of being seen, heard, less alone. And food is the fastest, easiest stand-in we've got.

The fix for this isn't more willpower. It's recognizing when the craving is for connection, and then—this is the hard part—actually reaching out. Texting a friend. Calling your sister. Joining a group where people show up in person and do something together that isn't eating. It feels awkward at first, especially if you've gotten used to soothing yourself in isolation. But the dopamine hit from genuine human connection is deeper and longer-lasting than anything you'll get from a bag of chips.

I know this because I've tested both. Extensively.

Let's get practical, because theory is useless if you can't apply it when you're standing in front of the fridge at 9 p.m. with your hand on the door handle.

When the craving hits, here's the sequence that actually works:

First: Pause. Don't try to resist. Don't white-knuckle it. Just stop for ten seconds. Literally count to ten. This alone will cut impulsive eating by a third, maybe more, because half of stress eating happens on autopilot. You're not deciding to eat; you're just eating. The pause forces a decision.

Second: Breathe. I know this sounds like wellness nonsense, but there's real physiology here. Deep breathing activates your parasympathetic nervous system—the part of your nervous system that tells your body the threat has passed and it's safe to stand down. Cortisol starts to drop. Your heart rate slows. The panic-driven urgency of the craving loses some of its grip.

Inhale for a count of four. Hold for a beat. Exhale for a count of six. Do this three times. If you're still craving food after that, at least now you're making a choice instead of running a script.

Third: Ask the question. *Am I hungry, or am I trying to feel something else?* Be honest. If you're hungry, eat. If you're not, name what you're actually feeling. Stressed. Lonely. Bored. Pissed off. Sad. Whatever it is, name it. Because once you name it, you can address it. And once you address it, food stops being the only option.

Fourth: Choose the real solution. If you're stressed, what you need isn't calories—it's a release valve. Go for a walk. Do twenty jumping jacks. Call someone and vent. Yell into a pillow. Cry if you need to. If you're lonely, reach out. Text someone. Scroll less, talk more. If you're bored, find something that engages your brain in a way that isn't food. Read. Draw. Build something. Learn something. Do a puzzle. Anything that asks your brain to focus on something other than the discomfort you're trying to avoid.

I'm not saying this will work every time. It won't. There will be days when you're too tired, too overwhelmed, too done to do anything but eat the thing and move on. That's fine. The goal isn't perfection. The goal is to catch yourself more often than you don't. To build the reflex of pausing, noticing, choosing.

Over time, that reflex gets stronger. The circuit rewires. You start reaching for the walk before the snack. You start calling the friend before opening the fridge. And the cravings—they don't disappear, but they lose their urgency. They become something you notice instead of something that controls you.

Let me tell you about someone who actually did this, because I think real examples matter more than hypotheticals.

Oprah Winfrey has talked openly for years about her struggles with weight and emotional eating, and one of the things she's said that stuck with me is this: she used to eat to numb feelings she didn't want to feel. Not because she was hungry. Because feeling nothing was easier than feeling too much. And food—especially rich, comforting food—was the fastest route to numb.

What shifted for her wasn't a new diet plan. It was the realization that the weight wasn't the problem. The weight was the *symptom*. The problem was that she was trying to bury feelings instead of processing them, and food was the shovel. Once she started addressing the feelings directly—through therapy, through honest conversations, through sitting with discomfort instead of smothering it—the eating patterns started to change. Not overnight. Not perfectly. But they changed.

I bring this up because I think we've been sold a lie about weight loss. We've been told it's about calories in, calories out. About discipline and meal plans and hitting the gym five days a week. And sure, those things matter on a mechanical level. But if the reason you're overeating is because you're drowning in cortisol and dopamine is the only life raft you've got, no amount of calorie counting is going to fix that. You have to address the *why* before the *what* will stick.

The why, for most of us, is some combination of stress and loneliness. We're working too much, sleeping too little, and spending too many hours in front of screens instead of across from actual human beings. We've built lives that are impressive on paper and utterly depleting in practice. And food is the cheapest, fastest way to feel a little bit better, a little bit less alone, a little bit rewarded for making it through another day.

So here's what I want you to sit with: What would it look like to actually address the stress instead of numbing it? To build real connections instead of substituting them with snacks? To let yourself feel lonely or sad or overwhelmed without immediately rushing to cover it up?

It's uncomfortable. I'm not going to lie to you and say it's easy or pleasant. Sitting with discomfort feels like exactly what it sounds like—uncomfortable. But discomfort doesn't kill you. And on the other side of it, there's something better than the fleeting relief of a dopamine hit. There's actual peace. Actual connection. Actual rest.

You don't have to overhaul your entire life tomorrow. You don't have to become a meditation guru or delete all the sugar from your house or start journaling your feelings every morning at dawn. You just have to start catching yourself. Start pausing. Start asking the question. Start choosing, even just once in a while, the thing that actually solves the problem instead of the thing that just makes it quieter for a minute.

I'm still working on this. I'll probably always be working on this. The difference is, now I know what I'm working on. It's not willpower. It's not discipline. It's the ability to notice what I'm really craving—calm, connection, relief—and to find it somewhere other than the bottom of a bag.

And you know what's wild? The more I practice this, the less I actually want the food. Not because I've trained myself to resist it, but because the craving itself is quieter. My baseline stress is lower. My cortisol isn't spiking six times a day. I'm not constantly in fight-or-flight mode, scrambling for dopamine anywhere I can find it.

Which brings me to what's coming next. Because stress doesn't just drive cravings. It doesn't just make you reach for comfort food. It rewires the way you think. The way you perceive threats. The way you make decisions. When cortisol runs high for long enough, your brain starts treating *everything* like an emergency. And that constant state of alarm doesn't just make you tired. It makes you sick.

We'll get into that in the next chapter. For now, I want you to try something small. The next time a craving hits, don't fight it. Just pause. Breathe. Ask the question. Notice what happens. Notice whether the craving is still there after ten seconds of breath. Notice what you're actually feeling underneath the urge to eat.

That noticing—that's where the shift begins.

The trap doesn't just hijack your body. It hijacks the voice in your head—the one that sounds rational, that gives you reasons, that tells you this time is different.

You know that voice. It's the one that says, "You've had a hard day. You deserve this." Or, "You've been good all week. One won't hurt." Or, "You're too stressed to cook. Just get takeout this once."

That voice isn't you. It's cortisol.

And here's what makes it so insidious: it doesn't *sound* like stress. It sounds like self-care. It sounds like permission. It sounds like a friend giving you reasonable advice. But what it's really doing is steering you toward the exact behaviors that keep the trap locked tight.

This is one of the most misunderstood parts of stress eating. We think of cravings as irrational impulses—something we should be able to resist with willpower. But when cortisol is elevated, your cravings come packaged in logic. They come with justifications. They come with a narrative that makes perfect sense in the moment.

Because cortisol doesn't just change what you want. It changes how you think.

When your stress system is activated, your prefrontal cortex—the part of your brain responsible for planning, decision-making, and self-control—gets temporarily downregulated. Blood flow shifts away from the thinking brain and toward the survival brain. Your amygdala, the emotional center, gets louder. Your hippocampus, which helps you remember past consequences, gets quieter.

What that means in practice is this: when you're stressed, you're not thinking clearly. You're not making long-term decisions. You're making short-term survival decisions. And in that state, the cookie isn't just a cookie. It's relief. It's safety. It's the fastest route back to calm.

Your brain doesn't care that you'll regret it later. Later doesn't exist when your nervous system thinks you're in danger.

So the voice in your head that says, "Just this once," isn't lying to you. It genuinely believes that eating will help. Because in that moment, with cortisol running the show, eating *does* help. It gives you a hit of dopamine. It shifts your nervous system out of fight-or-flight, even if only for a few minutes. It creates the illusion of control in a moment when everything else feels chaotic.

The problem is, it's a short-term solution to a long-term problem. And the more you use food to manage stress, the more your brain learns to associate stress with eating. The pathway gets stronger. The craving becomes automatic. And the voice becomes louder.

This is what I mean when I say the trap hijacks your mind. It doesn't just make you hungry. It makes you believe the hunger is reasonable. It gives you permission. It builds a case. And because it's happening inside your own head, in your own voice, you assume it's coming from you.

But it's not. It's coming from a stress system that's trying to protect you in the only way it knows how.

Let me give you an example. A client of mine—let's call her Maria—came to me because she couldn't stop eating at night. She'd have a perfectly reasonable dinner, feel satisfied, and then, around nine o'clock, the cravings would start. Ice cream. Chips. Leftover pizza. Whatever was in the house.

She'd tried everything. Meal prep. Earlier dinners. Not keeping snacks in the house. Nothing worked. And the voice in her head was relentless. "You didn't eat enough at dinner. You need more protein. Your blood sugar's low. You're not sleeping well, so your body needs extra fuel."

All of it sounded reasonable. All of it sounded true. And yet, when we actually tracked her intake, she was eating plenty. Her blood sugar was fine. Her dinners were balanced. So what was driving the cravings?

We started looking at her evenings. And here's what we found: every night, after her kids went to bed, Maria would sit down with her laptop and catch up on work emails. She didn't think of it as stressful. She thought of it as "getting things done." But her body didn't care what she called it. Her body registered the emails—the deadlines, the demands, the unfinished tasks—as threats. And it responded the way it always does: with cortisol.

Within twenty minutes of opening her inbox, her stress hormones would rise. Her heart rate would increase. Her nervous system would shift into high alert. And her brain, trying to bring her back to baseline, would start scanning for a quick fix.

Enter the cravings.

The voice that told her she was hungry wasn't wrong, exactly. Her body *was* asking for something. But it wasn't asking for food. It was asking for safety. It was asking for a break from the perceived threat. And because Maria had spent years using food to soothe herself after stressful days, her brain had learned to translate that need for safety into a need for ice cream.

Once we identified the pattern, the solution became obvious: she didn't need to change her diet. She needed to change her evenings. We created a new rule: no work email after dinner. Instead, she'd spend that time reading, stretching, or watching something light. Within two weeks, the nighttime cravings disappeared.

Not because she suddenly developed more willpower. But because we removed the trigger.

That's the thing about cortisol-driven cravings. They're not a character flaw. They're not a sign of weakness. They're a signal. And once you learn to read the signal, you can start responding to it in a way that actually addresses the root cause instead of just silencing the alarm.

But here's where it gets tricky. Because cortisol doesn't just create cravings in the moment. It also creates cravings in advance. It primes your brain to expect stress and to preemptively reach for food as a buffer.

This is what researchers call "anticipatory eating." And it's one of the sneakiest ways the trap operates.

Here's how it works. Let's say you have a stressful meeting coming up at two o'clock. Your conscious mind might not be worried about it yet. But your unconscious mind—the part that's always scanning for threats—registers it. And hours before the meeting even starts, your cortisol levels begin to rise.

Not a lot. Just enough to shift your baseline. Just enough to make you a little more reactive, a little more vigilant, a little more primed for danger.

And what does your brain do in response? It starts looking for ways to protect you. One of those ways is eating.

So at noon, even though you're not particularly hungry, you find yourself craving something heavy. Something filling. Something that will give you a sense of groundedness before you walk into that conference room. You tell yourself it's because you need energy. You tell yourself you didn't eat enough at breakfast. You tell yourself it's better to eat now than to be distracted by hunger during the meeting.

And all of that might be true. But the real reason you're eating isn't hunger. It's stress. Your body is trying to build a buffer. It's trying to shore up your reserves before the perceived threat arrives.

The problem is, the buffer doesn't work. You eat the sandwich, the chips, the cookie. You feel full. Maybe you even feel a little sluggish. And then you go into the meeting, and your stress levels rise anyway. Because the food didn't actually solve the problem. It just gave your brain something to do while it waited for the problem to arrive.

This is one of the reasons why stress eating feels so frustrating. You're not even enjoying the food. You're eating it preemptively, almost defensively, as if building a wall between yourself and the thing you're dreading. And then the thing happens anyway, and you're left feeling overfull, regretful, and no less stressed than you were before.

The trap has you coming and going. It makes you eat when you're stressed. It makes you eat when you're *about to be* stressed. And it makes you eat after the stress is over, as a reward for having survived.

Every stage of the cycle reinforces the next. And every time you use food to manage your emotional state, you're teaching your brain that food is the solution. Which means the next time stress shows up, your brain will reach for food even faster.

This is how habits form. Not through conscious choice, but through repetition. Your brain is a pattern-recognition machine. It notices what you do when you're stressed, and it files that away as useful information. The more often you pair stress with eating, the stronger that association becomes. Until eventually, the mere *feeling* of stress is enough to trigger a craving, even if there's no rational reason to eat.

And here's the kicker: once that pattern is established, it doesn't need much to activate it. You don't have to be in full-blown crisis mode. You don't have to be having the worst day of your life. All it takes is a minor stressor—a difficult conversation, a tight deadline, a frustrating commute—and your brain will pull the lever. Stress equals food. Food equals relief. The loop is automatic.

This is why willpower doesn't work. You're not fighting a craving. You're fighting a learned survival response. And your survival brain is always going to win that fight, because its job is to keep you alive. It doesn't care about your goals. It doesn't care about your waistline. It cares about making the bad feeling go away, as quickly as possible.

So what do you do?

You stop fighting the craving and start investigating it.

You start asking: *What is this craving actually trying to tell me?*

Because here's the truth: cravings aren't random. They're not meaningless. They're information. And if you can learn to decode them, you can start responding to your body's needs in a way that actually works.

Let's go back to the basics. When cortisol rises, your body is looking for three things: safety, energy, and soothing. Food provides all three, which is why it's such a common go-to. But food isn't the only way to meet those needs. And in most cases, it's not even the best way.

Safety can come from connection. From a five-minute conversation with someone you trust. From stepping outside and feeling the sun on your face. From putting your hand on your chest and reminding your nervous system that you're okay.

Energy can come from rest. From a short walk. From drinking water. From stepping away from the screen and giving your brain a break.

Soothing can come from music. From stretching. From a hot shower. From anything that signals to your body that the threat has passed and it's safe to relax.

The problem is, we've been conditioned to reach for food first. Because food is fast. It's reliable. It's always available. And it works, at least temporarily.

But when you start paying attention to what's underneath the craving—when you start asking, *What do I actually need right now?*—you create space for a different response. You give yourself the chance to meet the real need, instead of just masking it.

This doesn't mean the cravings will disappear overnight. It doesn't mean you'll never reach for food when you're stressed. But it does mean you'll start to notice the pattern. You'll start to see the gap between the feeling and the action. And in that gap, you have a choice.

That's where the power is. Not in resisting the craving, but in understanding it. Not in fighting your body, but in listening to it.

Because your body isn't trying to sabotage you. It's trying to protect you. And the cravings, as frustrating as they are, are its way of saying, *Something here isn't working. Something here needs to change.*

The trap wants you to believe the problem is you. That you're broken. That you lack discipline. That if you just tried harder, ate cleaner, stuck to the plan, everything would be fine.

But the problem isn't you. The problem is the system. The problem is a nervous system stuck in overdrive, flooding your body with stress hormones, and a brain doing its best to cope with a threat that never actually goes away.

You can't willpower your way out of that. But you can change the conditions that keep it active.

You can start by recognizing that stress eating isn't a moral failure. It's a biological response. And once you stop judging yourself for it, you can start getting curious about it. You can start noticing the patterns. The triggers. The times of day when it's worst. The situations that set it off.

You can start treating your cravings like clues instead of crimes.

And here's what you'll find, if you start paying attention: the cravings aren't consistent. They're not random, but they're not constant either. They have rhythms. They have triggers. They show up in predictable ways, at predictable times, in response to predictable stressors.

Which means they're changeable.

If you know what's triggering the craving, you can start addressing the trigger. If you know what need the craving is trying to meet, you can start meeting that need in a different way. If you know what your body is asking for underneath the urge to eat, you can start giving it what it actually wants.

This is the shift I'm talking about. Not from eating to not eating. But from unconscious reaction to conscious response. From being controlled by the cravings to understanding them. From feeling trapped to feeling curious.

It's not a quick fix. It's not a ten-day reset. It's a practice. And like any practice, it gets easier the more you do it.

But it starts with one simple act: pausing.

The next time a craving hits, don't fight it. Don't judge it. Don't try to push it away. Just pause. Take a breath. And ask yourself: *What am I actually feeling right now?*

Not what you think you should be feeling. Not what makes sense. Just what's true.

Are you tired? Overwhelmed? Lonely? Anxious? Bored? Frustrated? Angry? Sad?

Name it. Out loud, if you can. Because naming the feeling takes it out of your body and puts it into language. And once it's in language, your thinking brain can start working with it.

You don't have to fix the feeling. You don't have to make it go away. You just have to acknowledge it. Because that acknowledgment—that moment of seeing what's really happening—breaks the automatic loop. It creates space between the trigger and the response. And in that space, you have options.

You might still eat. That's okay. But you'll eat consciously, with awareness, instead of unconsciously, on autopilot. And that awareness, over time, changes everything.

Because once you see the pattern, you can't unsee it. Once you understand what's driving the cravings, you can't pretend it's just about food anymore. And once you realize that your body is trying to help you, not sabotage you, you can start working *with* it instead of against it.

That's what this chapter is really about. Not cravings. But the deeper connection between what you feel and what you eat. Between the stress you carry and the choices you make. Between the life you're living and the body you're living it in.

The cortisol trap doesn't just make you crave sugar. It makes you crave relief. And until you find a way to give your body the relief it's asking for—real relief, not just a temporary distraction—the cravings will keep coming back.

But here's the good news: relief is possible. Safety is possible. Calm is possible. Not someday, when your life is less stressful, but right now, in the middle of everything.

It starts with understanding that the craving isn't the enemy. The craving is the messenger. And the message is simple: *Your nervous system needs support.*

Not more rules. Not more restriction. Not more discipline.

Support.

Rest. Connection. Play. Movement. Touch. Laughter. Sunlight. Sleep. All the things that tell your body it's safe. All the things that bring your stress levels down and give your system a chance to reset.

These aren't luxuries. They're necessities. And when they're missing, your body will keep reaching for food to fill the gap.

So if you want to change your relationship with cravings, start by changing your relationship with stress. Start by asking: *What would it take for me to feel safe in my own body?*

Not perfect. Not problem-free. Just safe.

Because that's what your body is asking for, every time a craving hits. It's asking for permission to relax. It's asking for a break from the constant vigilance, the constant doing, the constant pushing through.

It's asking you to stop treating your life like an emergency.

And the moment you do—the moment you give your body what it actually needs—the cravings start to lose their grip. Not because you've beaten them, but because you've listened to them. Not because you've become stronger, but because you've become kinder.

The trap doesn't break through force. It breaks through awareness. Through curiosity. Through the willingness to see what's really happening, underneath the surface, beneath the noise.

And once you see it, everything changes.

Chapter 3: Chapter 3: Mind Over Matter

I was standing in my kitchen at 11:47 PM on a Wednesday, holding a jar of almond butter and a spoon, when I realized I wasn't hungry. Not even a little bit. I'd eaten dinner three hours earlier—a proper dinner, vegetables and everything—and my stomach felt fine. But my *chest* didn't.

I'd just gotten off a call with my publisher. Nothing bad, really. Just the usual tightening of a deadline, a request to rework a chapter, the kind of professional pressure that's supposed to feel normal when you've chosen a career that runs on other people's schedules. And yet there I was, spooning almond butter directly into my mouth like some kind of feral raccoon, trying to eat my way out of a feeling that had nothing to do with food.

The thing that stopped me wasn't willpower. I've never had much of that, honestly. What stopped me was noticing the pattern. The same dance I'd done a hundred times: stress hits, body tightens, brain reaches for something to make it stop, hand moves toward the pantry without conscious thought. I'd become so efficient at this loop that I could execute it in under sixty seconds, no deliberation required.

And that's the trap, isn't it? Not the cortisol itself, but the automation. The way we've trained ourselves to outsource emotional regulation to whatever's within arm's reach—food, wine, scrolling, shopping, anything that offers the brief illusion of control when everything else feels like it's slipping sideways.

We've made a terrible cultural bargain over the last few decades. Somewhere along the way, chronic stress became a credential. Proof you're important, needed, in demand. The entrepreneur who brags about sleeping four hours a night. The parent who wears exhaustion like a merit badge. The employee who responds to emails at midnight to prove their dedication. We've mistaken the warning light for the dashboard itself.

I'm not exempt from this. Last month I caught myself telling a friend, with something close to *pride*, that I'd worked through the weekend to meet a deadline. As if my inability to set boundaries was somehow admirable. As if my body's stress response—elevated cortisol, disrupted sleep, that low-grade tension headache that settled behind my eyes—was just the cost of being a serious person doing serious work.

But here's what I've learned, slowly and with significant resistance: the body doesn't negotiate. It doesn't care about your deadlines, your ambitions, or your carefully constructed narrative about why *your* stress is different, more legitimate, more unavoidable than everyone else's. When stress becomes chronic, your body responds the same way it would to any other persistent threat. It floods your system with cortisol. It triggers cravings for calorie-dense foods—the same foods that would have helped your ancestors survive a famine or outrun a predator. Except you're not outrunning anything. You're sitting at a desk, or stuck in traffic, or lying in bed at 2 AM replaying an awkward conversation from six hours earlier.

The mechanism is ancient. The mismatch is modern.

Consider Simone Biles at the Tokyo Olympics in 2021. The whole world watched as the greatest gymnast in history withdrew from multiple events, citing mental health concerns. What most people remember is the decision itself—the headlines, the controversy, the debates about toughness and commitment. What got less attention was what she said afterward about *the twisties*, a phenomenon where a gymnast loses spatial awareness mid-air. Your mind and body disconnect. You can't trust your own proprioception. And trying to push through it doesn't make you brave; it makes you likely to land on your neck.

Biles didn't withdraw because she was weak. She withdrew because she'd developed enough self-awareness to recognize when her internal state had become dangerous. When the gap between what her mind was asking and what her body could safely deliver had grown too wide.

That gap—between trigger and response, between stimulus and action—is where everything changes.

Most of us live on autopilot. Stress triggers craving triggers consumption triggers temporary relief triggers more stress. The loop tightens until it feels like there's no space to maneuver, no moment of choice. But that's not actually true. The space exists. We've just trained ourselves not to see it.

Let me tell you what that space looks like in practice, because it's not some mystical state of enlightenment. It's disappointingly ordinary.

It's the three seconds between feeling your shoulders hunch up toward your ears and deciding whether to leave them there or take a breath and drop them.

It's noticing that you've checked your phone six times in the last ten minutes not because you're waiting for anything important, but because your nervous system is looking for a hit of novelty to distract from the low-level anxiety humming in the background.

It's standing in your kitchen at 11:47 PM with a jar of almond butter and actually *asking yourself* what you're doing, instead of just doing it.

The framework isn't complicated. In fact, I'm going to give it to you in one sentence: **Between every trigger and every response, there's a gap—and your freedom lives in widening it.**

That's it. That's the whole teaching. Everything else is just practice.

But the practice matters, because widening that gap goes against every instinct your stress response has spent millennia perfecting. Your body doesn't *want* you to pause. Pausing feels dangerous when you're wired for threat. The entire point of the stress response is to bypass conscious thought and get you *moving*—fight, flight, freeze, whatever keeps you alive.

Except most of our modern stressors don't require movement. They require patience, perspective, emotional regulation, the ability to sit with discomfort without immediately trying to fix it. And we've never been worse at that.

There's a reason professional athletes spend as much time training their minds as their bodies. You think LeBron James just shows up and plays basketball? The man has a meditation practice. He works with sports psychologists. He's built an entire infrastructure around managing his internal state, because he understands something most of us are still learning: peak performance isn't about eliminating stress. It's about not letting stress hijack your decision-making.

Same thing with military special forces. Navy SEALs don't go through hell week just to prove they're tough. They're learning to maintain cognitive function under extreme duress. They're practicing the gap—the ability to feel their heart rate spike, their adrenaline surge, their body scream at them to *do something*, and still make a clear-headed decision instead of a panicked one.

You don't need to be an Olympic athlete or a Navy SEAL for this to matter. You just need to be a human being trying to get through a normal week without letting your stress response sabotage your health, your relationships, and your long-term well-being.

Here's where it gets uncomfortable, though. And I mean this in the most literal sense: building your capacity to widen the gap *requires* discomfort. You can't learn to sit with anxiety without actually sitting with anxiety. You can't develop emotional resilience by constantly numbing yourself the moment things get hard.

I learned this the worst way possible, which is the only way most of us learn anything important. A few years ago I was going through a particularly rough patch—work stress, family stuff, the usual existential spiral about whether anything I was doing mattered. And I handled it the way I'd always handled stress: I got busier. Took on more projects. Filled every available minute with productivity. Told myself I didn't have time to fall apart.

My body had other plans. Three months in, I started getting chest pains. Not dramatic, cinematic heart-attack pains, but enough to make me nervous. Enough to send me to a cardiologist, who ran a bunch of tests and then told me, with the kind of gentle directness that makes you want to punch something, that there was nothing wrong with my heart. The problem was stress.

"So what do I do?" I asked.

"Stop," he said.

I laughed. Because obviously I couldn't just *stop*. I had deadlines. Responsibilities. People depending on me.

"Then don't stop," he said, shrugging. "But your body's going to make the decision for you eventually, and you probably won't like the timing."

He was right, of course. They always are, these people who tell you obvious things you don't want to hear.

The hardest part about widening the gap isn't the technique. The technique is straightforward: notice what you're feeling, name it, take a breath, choose a response that aligns with your actual values instead of your panic reflexes. Simple. Not easy, but simple.

The hardest part is dismantling the belief that you *deserve* to feel this way. That your stress is proof of your importance. That suffering equals virtue.

We've internalized this so deeply that self-compassion feels like weakness. Like you're letting yourself off the hook. Like you're giving yourself permission to be lazy, mediocre, less than you could be.

But that's exactly backward. Self-compassion isn't about lowering your standards. It's about recognizing that berating yourself into better behavior has never worked, not once in the entire history of human psychology, and maybe—just maybe—there's a different way.

Kristin Neff, the psychologist who's spent her career studying self-compassion, puts it this way: self-compassion is what you'd offer a good friend who was struggling. You wouldn't tell them to stop being so weak. You wouldn't list all their failures and shortcomings. You'd acknowledge that what they're going through is hard. You'd remind them that everyone struggles sometimes. And you'd offer support without judgment.

Now do that for yourself. Out loud if you need to. I'm serious—I've stood in my bathroom at 6 AM, looked at my own tired face in the mirror, and said out loud: "This is hard. You're doing your best. It's okay to struggle."

Did I feel ridiculous? Absolutely. Did it help? More than I wanted to admit.

Let's get practical, because theory without application is just mental decoration.

Tonight—or tomorrow, or whenever you next feel that familiar pull toward your comfort substance of choice—try this:

Stop. Physically stop moving. Don't reach for the food, the phone, the wine, whatever it is. Just stand there.

Breathe. Three deep breaths. In through your nose, slow exhale through your mouth. Not because breathing is magic, but because it gives your prefrontal cortex a few seconds to come back online.

Notice. What's happening in your body right now? Tight chest? Clenched jaw? Shallow breathing? Just observe it. Don't try to fix it yet. You're gathering data.

Name it. What's the feeling underneath the craving? Anxiety? Loneliness? Exhaustion? Boredom? Anger? It's probably not hunger, unless you haven't eaten in six hours. Be honest.

Choose. Now—and only now—decide what you actually need. Maybe it *is* food, and that's fine. But maybe it's a phone call. A walk. A glass of water. Ten minutes lying on the floor doing absolutely nothing. Permission to go to bed even though it's only 8 PM and you "should" be productive.

The point isn't to never eat comfort food again. The point is to stop doing it on autopilot. To reclaim that tiny sliver of choice that exists between trigger and response.

You're going to fail at this. Repeatedly. I still do, and I've been practicing for years.

Last week I ate an entire sleeve of cookies while staring at my laptop, barely tasting them, because I was anxious about a project deadline. I didn't notice, didn't name, didn't choose. I just executed the pattern.

And you know what I did afterward? I didn't spiral into shame. I didn't decide that I was broken or hopeless or that self-compassion was clearly a scam. I just noticed the pattern, shrugged, and tried again the next time.

Because here's the thing they don't tell you about building new habits: progress isn't linear. You don't go from zero to enlightened in six weeks. You stumble forward, backslide, stumble forward again. And the wins aren't dramatic. They're quiet. They're the day you catch yourself mid-reach and decide to take a walk instead. The night you feel the anxiety rising and choose to call a friend rather than pour a drink. The moment you notice the tightness in your chest and think, *Oh, there you are*, instead of trying to force it away.

Small victories. Repeated over time. Compounding into something that starts to look like resilience.

I'm thinking about my aunt Carol again, the one who baked oatmeal cookies when her husband lost his job. I mentioned her to illustrate a point earlier, but I didn't tell you the whole story.

Six months after that conversation, Carol's husband still hadn't found work. Their savings were nearly gone. She'd taken a job at a grocery store to keep the lights on—a job she was wildly overqualified for, at age fifty-three, after spending two decades building a career she'd had to abandon because they couldn't afford childcare when the kids were young.

And she was still baking. But now she was also walking. Every morning, before her shift started, she'd walk three miles around her neighborhood. Rain, snow, didn't matter. I asked her about it once, expecting some story about exercise or weight loss.

"It's the only time my brain shuts up," she said. "Everything else just feels like static. But when I'm walking, I'm just... here. Feet on the ground. One step, then another. It's the only thing that makes sense right now."

Carol wasn't trying to practice mindfulness. She'd probably never heard the term. She was just doing what humans have always done when everything else falls apart: finding the thing that anchors you. The rhythm that centers you. The small, repeatable action that reminds you that you're still here, still capable, still moving forward even when forward feels impossible.

That's what widening the gap actually looks like. It's not transcendent. It's not Instagram-worthy. It's just you, showing up for yourself in the smallest, most ordinary ways, until those ways become the foundation of something stronger.

One more thing before I leave you:

Connection trumps everything else I've talked about in this chapter. All the self-awareness and breathing techniques and mindful pausing in the world won't save you if you're trying to do this alone.

Brené Brown talks about "vulnerability hangovers"—that feeling you get after you've been honest with someone about your struggles, when you wake up the next day and think, *Oh god, I said too much, they're going to think I'm a mess.* But here's what she found in her research: the people who live the most resilient, wholehearted lives aren't the ones who've figured out how to avoid vulnerability. They're the ones who've found people they can be vulnerable *with.* People who won't flinch when you admit you're struggling. Who won't try to fix you or minimize your pain. Who'll just sit with you and say, *Yeah, this is hard.*

Those people are worth more than every self-help book ever written, including this one.

So tonight, after you've practiced noticing the gap, after you've taken your three breaths and named what you're feeling, I want you to reach out to one person. Not to perform competence. Not to prove you're fine. Just to connect. Tell them something true. Ask how they're really doing. Remind both of you that you're not alone in this.

Because the real antidote to the cortisol trap isn't willpower or discipline or some perfectly optimized morning routine. It's the bone-deep knowledge that you're allowed to struggle, that struggle doesn't mean failure, and that on the other side of that struggle—not above it, not around it, but *through* it—there's a version of you that's a little bit stronger, a little bit kinder, a little bit more capable of sitting with discomfort without immediately trying to eat it, drink it, or scroll it away.

The gap is there. It's always been there. You're just learning to see it.

And once you see it, you can't unsee it. That's both the gift and the burden of awareness. You'll notice the tightness in your chest before the argument starts. You'll catch the way your shoulders creep up toward your ears when you open your inbox. You'll feel the split-second decision point between snapping at your kid or taking one breath first.

None of this makes you calm. Let's be clear about that. Seeing the gap doesn't erase the gap. You're not suddenly going to float through life in a state of unshakeable zen, smiling beatifically at traffic jams and tax forms. You're still going to get angry, anxious, overwhelmed. You're still going to reach for your phone when you're bored, your credit card when you're sad, your old familiar stories when things get hard.

But here's what changes: you'll know you're doing it. And that tiny sliver of knowing—that microscopic pause between feeling and acting—is where your actual life happens. Not the life you're planning for when things calm down, not the life you'll live once you finally get your act together, but the life you're living *right now*, in the space between what happens and what you do about it.

Most of us spend years—decades, even—trying to eliminate that space. We want a tighter loop. Faster reflexes. More efficiency. We want to be the kind of person who doesn't have to think about doing the right thing, who just *does* it automatically. And there's nothing wrong with building good habits, with making the healthy choice the easy choice. But if you're trying to bypass the gap entirely, to short-circuit the moment of choice, you're trying to bypass your own humanity.

Because the gap is where change lives. It's where you get to decide who you are today, regardless of who you were yesterday. It's where the pattern can break. It's where the person you've been practicing being in therapy or in books or in quiet moments alone finally gets to show up in real time, in real life, with real stakes.

Your nervous system doesn't care about any of this, of course. Your amygdala isn't interested in your personal growth journey. It's got one job—keep you alive—and it's been doing that job for a very long time without your conscious input, thank you very much. So when it registers a threat, real or imagined, it's going to flood you with cortisol and adrenaline whether you've meditated that morning or not.

But you—the you that's reading this, the you that's aware of the gap—you get a vote. Not always. Not easily. But more often than you think. You get to notice the flood and say, "Okay. This is happening.

This is cortisol. This is my body trying to help me survive a threat that isn't actually there." And then, in the three seconds before you hit send on that email or slam that door or say the thing you can't unsay, you get to ask: *Is this who I want to be right now?*

Sometimes the answer is yes. Sometimes you're going to slam the door anyway, and that's fine. You're not a monk. But at least you'll be slamming it on purpose.

The kitchen clock read 11:47 PM—not late enough to be outrageous, not early enough to still be dinnertime, just that specific margin where the trap operates best.

Your thoughts can trap you. Your appetite can trap you. But there's one biological system cortisol commandeers that makes both of those worse, and you surrender to it every single night.

Chapter 4: Chapter 4: Sleep and Stress

Your sleep specialist doesn't talk to your GP, and your GP doesn't talk to your gastroenterologist. That's not negligence—it's how the system works. Which means when stress fractures your biology across three separate systems, you leave with three separate prescriptions and no one asking why they all showed up at once.

None of them—not one—asked about my work schedule.

It was the nurse practitioner, a tired-looking woman named Sarah who was covering for my GP during his vacation, who finally asked the question that unraveled everything. She was scanning my chart, frowning at the list of medications, when she looked up and said, "Have you considered that these might all be stress?"

I remember laughing. Actually laughing. Because of course I was stressed—who wasn't? But that was just... normal. That was life. That was proof I mattered, that I had responsibilities, that people needed me. The idea that stress could manifest as insomnia *and* weight gain *and* a knot in my stomach that felt like I'd swallowed a fist—that all three specialists had been treating symptoms of a single problem—struck me as almost absurd.

Sarah didn't laugh. She just closed the chart and said, "Your body doesn't care how important your deadlines are."

That sentence has stayed with me for years now. Because she was right. We've culturally elevated chronic stress into a credential—proof you're important, busy, needed. We wear our exhaustion like medals. I can't count the number of conversations I've had where someone's opener is, "God, I'm so slammed," delivered with a kind of pride, as though their overflowing calendar were evidence of worth rather than warning of collapse.

The body doesn't negotiate with ambition. It doesn't care about quarterly reports or book deadlines or the carefully curated image you're projecting on LinkedIn. It only understands one language: survival. And when you flood it with constant signals of threat—even self-imposed ones, even ones you've convinced yourself are voluntary—it responds the only way it knows how. It dumps cortisol into your system, preparing you to fight or flee from dangers that never actually arrive.

Here's what we forget: cortisol isn't the villain. In the right context, it's lifesaving. It's what gets you out of the burning building, what sharpens your focus during a genuine crisis. The problem is that your hypothalamus—the ancient, primitive part of your brain that governs this response—can't distinguish between a tiger and an overdue report. A looming deadline triggers the same cascade of stress hormones as an actual physical threat. Your heart rate spikes. Your digestion shuts down. Your immune system takes a backseat. And cortisol, which is supposed to spike briefly and then retreat, starts running the show 24/7.

That's when acute stress—the kind that saves your life—becomes chronic stress, the kind that quietly dismantles it.

Winston Churchill understood this, which might surprise you given his reputation as an indefatigable wartime leader. The man worked punishing hours during World War II, often through the night, coordinating strategy across multiple theaters of war. But he also took an afternoon nap every single day. Not occasionally. Not when he felt like it. Every day, without exception, usually around 3 PM. He'd change into pajamas, get into bed properly, and sleep for an hour or more.

When aides or military officials expressed surprise—or occasionally frustration, given the urgency of wartime decisions—Churchill was unapologetic. He insisted the nap didn't cost him time; it doubled his productive day. By sleeping in the afternoon, he could work effectively until two or three in the morning and still wake refreshed. "Nature must be taken in doses," he reportedly said. He didn't view rest as weakness or indulgence. He viewed it as strategic necessity.

What Churchill grasped intuitively, and what modern sleep science has confirmed, is that sustained performance requires deliberate restoration. You can't run a system at maximum capacity indefinitely. Something breaks. Usually several things at once.

For me, it was sleep that broke first.

The insomnia started gradually—an extra thirty minutes of lying awake here, an hour there. I'd tell myself it was fine, that I'd catch up on the weekend. Then the weekends came and I'd lie there, exhausted but wired, my mind churning through the same circular anxieties. I started drinking more coffee to compensate for the fatigue, which of course made the insomnia worse, which led to more coffee, until I was caught in a cycle I barely recognized as a cycle. It just felt like... life.

The weight gain baffled me more than it should have. I was eating less—genuinely less, not the self-deceiving less where you forget about the afternoon snacking. I'd started skipping breakfast because I wasn't hungry in the mornings, and lunch was often something grabbed between meetings. Dinner was the only real meal, and even that was frequently distracted, eaten while answering emails or reviewing edits. I should have been losing weight. Instead, my clothes were getting tighter, my face puffier in photos.

What I didn't understand then—what the GP didn't think to explain, or maybe didn't know himself—is that chronic cortisol elevation fundamentally alters your metabolism. It signals your body to store fat, particularly around your midsection, because from an evolutionary standpoint, ongoing stress means resources are scarce and you'd better hold onto every calorie you can. It doesn't matter that you're actually sitting at a desk, that the "stress" is psychological rather than physical. Your body is preparing for famine.

The stomach pain was the final piece, though I didn't connect it at first. It started as occasional discomfort after meals, a tightness that would fade after an hour or two. But it gradually became constant—a low-grade ache that sharpened when I was particularly anxious. I assumed it was something I was eating, tried cutting out dairy, then gluten, then caffeine (which lasted about four days before I caved). Nothing helped. The gastroenterologist did an endoscopy, found mild inflammation, and handed me the prescription for acid reducers.

Three doctors. Three diagnoses. Three prescriptions.

One problem.

The irony is that I was writing about stress at the time. I was literally researching the physiological impacts of cortisol dysregulation for this book, interviewing researchers and reading studies, while somehow maintaining a complete blind spot about my own situation. I knew intellectually that chronic stress suppressed immune function, disrupted digestion, interfered with sleep. I just didn't connect those abstract facts to my own concrete symptoms.

This is the trap. We're excellent at compartmentalizing. We convince ourselves that the tightness in our chest is indigestion, not the deadline looming. That the insomnia is just a rough patch, not a warning signal. That everyone feels this way, that it's normal, that pushing through exhaustion is what responsible adults do.

And then a nurse practitioner asks one simple question and the whole facade cracks open.

Here's what I wish someone had told me earlier: sleeplessness doesn't just make you tired. It amplifies cortisol, which makes you more reactive, more anxious, less able to regulate your emotions. Which makes it even harder to fall asleep the next night. You're not just tired; you're caught in a self-reinforcing spiral where each element strengthens the others.

Think of it as a triangle. At one corner is poor sleep. At another is elevated cortisol. At the third is increased stress reactivity—your lowered threshold for anxiety, irritation, overwhelm. Each corner feeds the other two. Less sleep means more cortisol. More cortisol means heightened stress response. Heightened stress response means worse sleep. Around and around.

Breaking the cycle requires interrupting it at any of those three points. But sleep is often the most accessible entry point, because it's the one element you have some direct control over—more control than you have over your body's cortisol production, anyway, and more control than you often have over external stressors.

I want to be clear: I'm not suggesting sleep is some magic cure that will dissolve all your problems. I'm not claiming that eight hours of rest will repair a toxic job or a failing relationship or systemic injustice. But it does give you a fighting chance. It gives you the cognitive bandwidth to make better decisions, the emotional resilience to handle setbacks, the physical energy to actually take action rather than just ruminating about it at 3 AM.

After Sarah's question—*have you considered these might all be stress?*—I went home and looked at my calendar. Really looked at it, not just the surface level of meetings and deadlines, but the deeper pattern. I was triple-booked most days. I'd stopped taking a real lunch break months earlier. I was checking email until midnight and often responding to messages before I'd even gotten out of bed in the morning. I'd convinced myself this was temporary, that once I got through this particular crunch period things would ease up.

But there was always another crunch period. There would always be another deadline, another urgent request, another reason to sacrifice sleep for productivity.

The shift for me started with one small, almost laughably simple change: I set an alarm for 10 PM. Not a wake-up alarm—a wind-down alarm. When it went off, I had to start my pre-sleep routine, no exceptions. No "just one more email." No "let me just finish this paragraph." The alarm meant I stopped.

At first, this felt impossible. Wasteful, even. I'd lie in bed, mentally cataloging everything I should be doing instead, feeling guilty for resting while work remained undone. My mind would race through tomorrow's agenda, replaying today's conversations, spinning out anxious scenarios about upcoming challenges.

But I kept at it. Because the alternative—the path I'd been on, the one leading to three specialists and a handful of prescriptions—wasn't sustainable. I was already seeing what that road led to, and it wasn't anywhere I wanted to go.

I started keeping a notebook by the bed. When an anxious thought surfaced, I'd jot it down—not to solve it, just to capture it so my brain would stop holding onto it. I started reading fiction before sleep instead of work-related material, something to shift my mental gears away from my own life. I experimented with temperature—it turns out I sleep better when the room is almost uncomfortably cool, around 65 degrees.

Some nights were better than others. There were still bouts of insomnia, still nights where I'd lie awake for hours despite doing everything "right." But gradually, over weeks and then months, the pattern shifted. I started falling asleep more easily. Staying asleep more consistently. Waking up feeling less like I'd been hit by a truck.

And the other symptoms—the weight, the stomach pain—began to ease without any other intervention. The fifteen pounds came off slowly, almost imperceptibly. The knot in my stomach loosened. I didn't need the Ambien or the metformin or the acid reducers. I needed to stop treating my body like a machine that could run indefinitely without maintenance.

You might be thinking this sounds too simple. That after everything you've tried—every sleep hack and meditation app and wellness trend—the answer can't possibly be just... prioritizing rest. It feels reductive, maybe even dismissive of the genuine complexity of your life.

But that's the thing. We overcomplicate this. We chase elaborate solutions while ignoring the foundational need sitting right in front of us. We act as though sleep is optional, a luxury we can defer until some imaginary future moment when life calms down and we have time to rest.

Life doesn't calm down. There is no perfect moment when all your obligations resolve and you're finally permitted to sleep. You have to claim that time, defend it, treat it as non-negotiable—not because you're lazy or weak, but because you're a biological organism with fundamental needs that don't vanish just because you're busy.

I'm still working on this, to be honest. There are weeks when I backslide, when I fall into old patterns of checking email late into the night or skipping my wind-down routine because I've convinced myself that this particular task is too urgent to wait until morning. And every time, I pay for it. Not immediately—that's part of what makes it so insidious—but gradually, as the sleep debt accumulates and the cortisol triangle begins tightening again.

The difference now is that I recognize what's happening. I can see the trap forming before I'm fully caught in it. And that awareness, that small shift in perspective, creates the possibility of a different choice.

So tonight—literally tonight, not some future version where you've cleared your calendar and your life is perfectly balanced—I want you to try something. Set a wind-down alarm. Pick a time that gives you a realistic shot at seven or eight hours of sleep, and when that alarm goes off, stop. Not in ten minutes. Not after you finish just one more thing. Stop.

You're not going to want to. Your brain will generate a dozen compelling reasons why tonight is different, why this particular task can't wait, why rest can be deferred just one more day. Those reasons will feel urgent and true.

But consider: what would happen if you treated sleep with the same seriousness you treat your other responsibilities? What if rest wasn't something you fit in around the edges of your life, but a foundation upon which everything else is built?

The work will still be there tomorrow. The emails will still need answering, the deadlines will still loom. But you'll face them with a nervous system that's had a chance to recalibrate, with cortisol levels that have actually dipped instead of remaining elevated around the clock. You'll make better decisions. You'll be more creative, more patient, more resilient.

Or you can keep doing what you've been doing. Keep pushing through exhaustion, keep wearing your sleeplessness like a badge of honor, keep waiting for life to slow down enough to permit rest.

Sarah's voice comes back to me in these moments: *Your body doesn't care how important your deadlines are.*

It doesn't. It only cares whether you're giving it what it needs to function. And right now, what it needs is for you to close your eyes and let go—not as an ending, but as the beginning of something different. Something sustainable.

The choice, as always, is yours. But the alarm is set. And when it goes off tonight, you'll have to decide which version of yourself you're becoming.

I walked out with three prescriptions in my bag, each one treating a different system, none of them talking to each other.

The kitchen clock read 11:47 PM—not late enough to be outrageous, not early enough to still be dinnertime, just that specific margin where the trap operates best. When you're exhausted and wired at the same time, your body starts making brutal choices about who to keep close and who to cut loose.

I sat at the table and looked at my phone. Twelve text messages. Four from my partner asking where I was. Three from a friend I'd been meaning to call back for two weeks. Two work emails that had somehow migrated into my personal inbox. One from my mother. One from the dentist. One group thread I'd muted six months ago that kept resurfacing like a bill collector.

I didn't open any of them.

This is what chronic elevation does to connection—it makes every interaction feel like a transaction you can't afford. The people who care about you start to register as demands. Their texts arrive as pings of obligation. Their voices on the phone sound like deadlines. And the worst part is knowing, even as it's happening, that you're pushing away exactly what you need most.

The research on this is unambiguous. Cortisol doesn't just make you tired or anxious or inflamed—it rewires how you perceive threat. And in a chronically activated system, the people closest to you start registering as part of the threat landscape. Not because they're dangerous, but because they require something from you: attention, presence, emotional bandwidth. Resources you no longer have.

I put the phone face-down and stared at the prescription bag.

One for the gut issues. One for the blood pressure. One for sleep, which the doctor had hesitated to prescribe but finally relented because "you need to break the cycle somehow." What she didn't say, but what we both understood, was that the cycle wasn't breaking on its own. It was tightening.

The sleep medication was a Z-drug, the kind that shows up in late-night infomercials with disclaimers about sleepwalking and amnesia and operating heavy machinery. I'd resisted for months because I didn't want to be the person who needed chemical intervention just to do what my body was supposed to do automatically. But exhaustion has a way of lowering your standards. You stop asking *should I* and start asking *how fast will this work.*

I took one pill out of the blister pack and set it on the counter. It was small, oblong, pale blue. Harmless-looking. The kind of thing that promised relief without explaining the cost.

Here's what they don't tell you in the fifteen-minute appointment: sleep medications don't fix the cortisol problem. They override it. They chemically suppress the arousal system long enough for you to lose consciousness, but they don't restore the natural rhythm. They don't teach your body how to downregulate on its own. They're a floor, not a foundation. And if you stay on them long enough, the floor becomes the ceiling.

But that night, sitting in my kitchen with a pulse that wouldn't settle and a mind that wouldn't stop inventory-checking every unfinished task, I didn't care about long-term architecture. I cared about making it to tomorrow without collapsing.

I swallowed the pill with tap water and waited.

The pharmaceutical intervention is seductive precisely because it's fast. You don't have to renegotiate your schedule or confront your boss or admit to anyone that you're operating past capacity. You just take the pill and let chemistry do what willpower couldn't. And for a few hours, it works. You sleep. You wake up. You function. The cycle continues.

What you don't notice, at least not right away, is that you're borrowing against a balance that's already overdrawn.

Twenty minutes later, I felt the edges soften. My thoughts started to drift instead of ricochet. The hum in my chest—the one that had been running since Tuesday—started to fade. I stood up, turned off the kitchen light, and walked upstairs with the kind of careful deliberation you use when you're already half-gone.

I didn't brush my teeth. Didn't check the locks. Didn't set an alarm. I just got into bed and let the chemical tide pull me under.

When I woke up seven hours later, I felt like I'd been awake the whole time.

This is the paradox of pharmacological sleep under chronic stress: you get the hours, but not the restoration. The architecture is wrong. REM gets suppressed. Deep sleep gets fragmented. You spend more time in light stages that don't do much except keep you technically unconscious. Your brain logs it as sleep. Your body doesn't.

And cortisol, which should be low at night and rising gently in the morning, stays elevated. Because the pill didn't fix what was driving it. It just put a weighted blanket over the alarm.

I reached for my phone. 6:18 AM. Four new emails. A calendar notification reminding me of a meeting I'd forgotten about. A news alert about something I didn't have the bandwidth to process. I swiped them all away and stared at the ceiling.

This is the moment where you're supposed to feel grateful. You slept. You made it through the night. You have another chance to get it right. But all I felt was dread.

Because I knew what came next.

The shower. The coffee. The commute. The inbox. The meetings that should have been emails and the emails that should have been resolved weeks ago. The performance of competence. The smile you paste on when someone asks how you're doing, because "I'm barely holding it together and medicating just to sleep" doesn't fit into the thirty-second exchange by the coffee machine.

You do it because stopping isn't an option. Because the mortgage doesn't care about your cortisol curve. Because your team is counting on you. Because admitting you're drowning feels like admitting you're weak, and weakness in this economy is a liability you can't afford.

So you get up. You perform. You push through. And every day, the cost gets a little higher.

The thing about chronic activation is that it's cumulative, not catastrophic. You don't collapse all at once. You erode. A little focus here. A little patience there. A relationship that used to feel easy starts to feel like work. A hobby that used to restore you starts to feel like another obligation. The margin between you and breaking gets thinner, and you stop noticing because you're too busy trying not to break.

By the time you realize how far gone you are, you've been running on fumes for months.

I got out of bed and looked at myself in the bathroom mirror. Same face. Same eyes. But something behind them had dimmed. Not depression, exactly—though that was probably lurking nearby. More like the specific fatigue that comes from spending every waking moment managing a system that's supposed to manage itself.

I thought about the prescriptions downstairs. The one for sleep I'd already started. The one for blood pressure I was supposed to take every morning. The one for gut issues I'd been putting off because adding another pill felt like admitting defeat.

This is what the trap looks like from the inside. Not a single catastrophic failure, but a cascade of small compensations that eventually become your baseline. You don't notice you're declining because you're too busy managing the decline.

The research literature has a term for this: allostatic load. It's the cumulative wear and tear on your body from chronic stress. Every time cortisol spikes and doesn't fully resolve, you add to the load. Every night of fragmented sleep. Every skipped meal replaced with coffee. Every conflict you swallow instead of addressing. Every boundary you don't set because setting it feels harder than enduring the violation.

The load builds. And unlike acute stress, which mobilizes and then releases, allostatic load just accumulates. It shows up as inflammation. As insulin resistance. As vascular stiffness. As immune dysregulation. As the gut issues and blood pressure problems and sleep disruption that send you to the doctor in the first place.

And here's the cruelest part: by the time it shows up in labs and symptoms, you've been loading the system for years.

I turned on the shower and waited for the water to heat up. Steam filled the small bathroom, fogging the mirror until I disappeared. I stood under the water longer than I needed to, letting it run over my shoulders, my neck, the place between my shoulder blades that hadn't fully relaxed in what felt like months.

For a moment, I thought about what it would take to actually fix this. Not manage it. Fix it.

It would mean saying no. A lot. To projects, to people, to opportunities that looked good on paper but cost more than they paid. It would mean disappointing people who expected me to keep showing up the way I always had. It would mean admitting that I'd overcommitted, overextended, overestimated my capacity to carry it all.

It would mean renegotiating my entire life.

I turned off the water and reached for a towel.

The problem with living inside the trap is that leaving it requires a kind of clarity and energy you don't have while you're trapped. You need rest to make the decisions that will allow you to rest. You need space to create space. You need margin to protect margin. And when you're running on empty, every decision defaults to survival mode: what gets me through today, not what gets me out of this.

This is why intervention often feels impossible. Not because the steps are complicated—they're not—but because executing them requires resources you've already spent.

So you stay. You compensate. You medicate. You push through. And the load keeps building.

I got dressed and went downstairs. The prescription bag was still on the counter where I'd left it. I took out the blood pressure medication and read the label. *Take one tablet by mouth every morning.* Simple. Clinical. No mention of what it meant to need it at forty-three.

I swallowed it dry and put the bottle next to the coffee maker so I wouldn't forget tomorrow.

This is the compromise you make when you can't afford the real solution. You treat the symptoms and hope the underlying problem resolves on its own. You know it won't, but hope is cheaper than rearranging your entire existence.

The gut medication stayed in the bag. I told myself I'd start it tomorrow.

I made coffee and sat at the kitchen table with my laptop. The inbox had grown while I slept—forty-seven new messages, twelve of them flagged urgent. I opened the first one and felt my heart rate tick up before I'd even finished the subject line.

This is the other thing cortisol does: it makes everything feel urgent. Your threat-detection system loses calibration. A colleague's mildly terse email reads like a reprimand. A delayed response feels like rejection. A full inbox becomes a referendum on your competence. The line between actual crisis and perceived crisis dissolves, and you start responding to everything with the same elevated activation.

You become the crisis you're trying to manage.

I closed the laptop and stared at the coffee. It was too hot to drink, but I tried anyway, burning my tongue in the process. The pain was sharp and immediate and, in a strange way, clarifying. At least it was real. At least I could locate it.

The rest of the day passed the way these days always do. Meetings that could have been emails. Emails that required meetings. A project timeline that had shifted again, compressing the deadline without reducing the scope. A conversation with my manager that was framed as a check-in but felt like a performance review. A lunch I ate at my desk while proofreading a document I should have finished last week.

By three PM, the medication I'd taken that morning had worn off, and I could feel my pulse in my throat again.

By five PM, I was staring at my screen without reading it.

By six PM, I was still at my desk, not because I was being productive, but because leaving felt like giving up.

This is what chronic activation does to time. It warps it. Hours stretch and compress simultaneously. You're always behind and always rushing, but nothing ever gets finished. The to-do list regenerates faster than you can clear it. And every evening, you carry the unfinished work home with you—not as tasks, but as ambient dread.

The technical term is "cognitive load." The lived experience is: you never stop working, even when you're not working.

I finally shut the laptop at seven-thirty and drove home in traffic that had thinned but not cleared. The same route I took every day. The same exits. The same stretch of highway where the pavement was bad and your tires made that specific hum that used to annoy me but now barely registered.

I pulled into the driveway and sat in the car for a moment before going inside.

This is the buffer. The transitional space between work-you and home-you. Except when you're chronically activated, there is no home-you. There's just work-you in a different location, still wired, still scanning for threats, still unable to fully arrive.

I walked in and my partner looked up from the couch. "Hey. How was your day?"

"Fine."

It wasn't fine. It hadn't been fine in months. But "fine" is what you say when the real answer is too complicated to unpack before dinner.

They nodded and went back to their phone, and I felt the familiar pang of guilt mixed with relief. Guilt because I knew I was withdrawing. Relief because engaging felt like one more thing I didn't have the capacity for.

We used to talk. Real conversations, not transactional updates. We used to laugh about things that weren't funny. We used to sit in the same room without needing to fill the silence. But somewhere in the last year, that had evaporated. Not all at once. Just slowly, imperceptibly, the way snow melts when you're not looking.

I couldn't pinpoint when it happened. There was no inciting incident, no fight, no betrayal. Just the slow erosion of presence. The nights I stayed up working instead of coming to bed. The weekends I spent catching up instead of catching up with them. The conversations I cut short because I was too tired to listen, too overloaded to care.

Cortisol doesn't just disrupt sleep. It disrupts attachment. It makes you unavailable, even when you're physically present. It turns the people you love into obstacles between you and the relief you're chasing.

And the worst part is, you don't mean to. You're not trying to hurt anyone. You're just trying to survive. But survival mode doesn't leave room for connection. It's a single-player game. And everyone else becomes collateral.

I opened the fridge and stared at the contents without seeing them. Leftovers I didn't remember making. Vegetables that had gone soft. A carton of milk that was probably expired. I closed the door and ordered takeout instead.

Dinner was quiet. We ate in front of the TV, watching something neither of us cared about, filling the space with noise so we didn't have to fill it with words. I finished first and took my plate to the sink, rinsed it, and left it there instead of putting it in the dishwasher.

Small things. Tiny erosions. The kind of negligence that doesn't matter once but compounds over time.

I went upstairs and got into bed at nine-thirty, even though I wasn't tired. I just wanted the day to be over.

I reached for the sleep medication on the nightstand. The bottle was still new, twenty-nine pills left. Enough for a month, assuming I only took one per night, assuming I didn't build tolerance, assuming this was temporary.

None of those assumptions were safe.

I took the pill and lay down, staring at the ceiling, waiting for the chemical tide. My mind did what it always did—ran through the day's mistakes, tomorrow's demands, the growing list of things I'd left undone. I tried to stop it, tried to focus on my breath, tried all the things the internet says to try when you can't shut your brain off.

None of it worked. It never does when your nervous system is convinced that vigilance is survival.

Twenty minutes later, the edges softened again, and I drifted.

I don't remember my dreams, but I remember waking up at two AM with my heart pounding, drenched in sweat, convinced I'd forgotten something catastrophic. I checked my phone. No new emails. No missed calls. No evidence of disaster. Just the same low-level dread I'd gone to bed with, now amplified by interrupted sleep and residual medication.

I lay there for an hour, trying to fall back asleep, knowing I wouldn't.

By three AM, I gave up and went downstairs. The house was dark and silent, and I moved through it carefully, trying not to wake my partner, trying not to acknowledge that this was becoming routine.

I sat at the kitchen table with my laptop and opened my email. Seventeen new messages since I'd last checked. I answered three of them, not because they were urgent, but because doing something felt better than lying in bed doing nothing.

This is the trap at its tightest: when rest feels like failure and productivity feels like proof of worth. When you've been running so long that stopping feels more dangerous than continuing. When the system designed to protect you has turned against you, and you're too tired to notice.

I worked until four-thirty, then went back to bed and lay there until my alarm went off at six.

Two hours later, I was back at my desk, pretending yesterday hadn't happened, pretending today would be different, pretending I had this under control.

The gut medication was still in the bag. I still hadn't started it. I told myself I'd start it tomorrow.

Chapter 5: Chapter 5: Social Support

I came home after what I'd call a normal workday and snapped at my partner for leaving dishes in the sink. Not annoyed—genuinely furious, voice shaking, that tight-chest rage you feel when something small becomes the thing you're ready to burn the house down over.

My partner gave me the same look Darlene had given those fries weeks ago—not judgment, but recognition of someone caught in something they couldn't name.

I had.

The dishes weren't the problem. I'd been running on cortisol fumes for weeks, sleeping poorly, eating worse, and my body had been screaming at me in every language except words. The dishes were just the first object in range when the pressure valve finally blew.

Here's what I didn't understand at the time, what I couldn't see because I was too deep inside it: isolation amplifies cortisol the way a closed room amplifies heat. You think you're handling it—work stress, money stress, the ambient hum of modern life—but your nervous system is keeping score in a language you can't hear until the numbers get so high the system just fails. And when you're going it alone, the score climbs faster than you think, faster than feels fair.

This isn't some soft emotional claim about needing people to make you feel better. It's physiology. When you're chronically stressed and isolated, your body interprets that combination as a threat signal older than language: *You're alone. No backup. No tribe. Danger must be close.* Your adrenal glands respond the only way they know how. Cortisol stays elevated because your system has no social cues telling it the threat has passed, that the predator moved on, that you can stand down now. A text from a friend won't cure your insomnia. But the complete absence of any social anchor—the bone-deep sense that no one knows what you're carrying—makes the cycle worse in ways you won't notice until you're snapping at someone you love over a bowl in the sink.

Let me give you a real example, not some composite case I'm dressing up to make a point. Matthew McConaughey talked in his memoir *Greenlights* about a period in his late twenties when he'd become famous fast, faster than he knew how to process, and felt completely unmoored. No one around him understood what he was going through. He didn't trust that anyone *could* understand. The people close to him now wanted something from him—his time, his attention, his brand. He described lying awake at night in houses that weren't his, replaying conversations, second-guessing every choice, his mind spinning faster the quieter the room got. The loneliness wasn't about being physically alone. It was about being surrounded by people and still feeling like no one actually saw him.

What finally shifted wasn't a breakthrough or a technique or a therapist giving him the magic reframe. It was reconnecting with old friends from Texas who'd known him before the fame, people who didn't need him to perform or explain himself, who'd give him shit the same way they always had. That re-grounding—being around people who saw him as a whole person, not a celebrity or a resource—gave his nervous system permission to stand down. To stop treating every interaction like a performance he could fail.

That's the mechanism most people miss. Social connection doesn't just make you *feel* better in some vague, hand-wavy emotional sense. It regulates your stress response at the hormonal level, the same level where cortisol is wreaking havoc on your sleep.

When you're with people you trust, people who aren't evaluating you or extracting something from you, your body reads safety. Cortisol drops. Oxytocin rises. Your heart rate variability improves, which is one of the better measures we have of how flexibly your nervous system can shift between stress and recovery. You sleep better that night not necessarily because you talked through your problems—though sometimes that helps—but because your body got the signal it needed: *You're not alone in this. The tribe is here. You can rest.*

Now here's where I need to interrupt myself, because I'm making this sound clean and linear and obvious, and it's not. I *know* this intellectually. I've read the research, I've written about it, I've explained the mechanism to other people. And I still default to isolating when I'm stressed. It's hardwired in me, maybe in you too. When cortisol spikes, the instinct isn't to reach out. It's to withdraw, to manage it privately, to not "burden" anyone with what you're going through. Which is exactly backward, exactly the move that keeps you trapped. The times I've slept worst in my life weren't the times when the most was objectively going wrong. They were the times I tried to white-knuckle it alone, convinced that asking for help or even admitting I was struggling was a sign I couldn't handle my own life.

So if you're reading this and thinking, "Yeah, but I don't *want* to talk to anyone when I'm stressed"—I get it. That's the trap. The stress response itself makes you want to isolate, which keeps the stress response active, which makes you want to isolate more. It's a loop that tightens until you can't remember what it felt like to *not* be in it. You have to override the instinct, not because it feels good in the moment—it won't—but because the alternative, staying in the loop, will eventually break something in you that's hard to fix.

Let's talk practically, because vague principles don't help at 2 a.m. when you're lying there with your heart racing and your mind spinning. What does "social support" actually mean in that moment? It doesn't mean you need to call someone at 2 a.m.—though if you have that person, the kind who'd pick up and not resent you for it, hold onto them like gold. It means you've built enough connection during daylight hours that your nervous system has evidence, accumulated over time, that you're not alone. The support doesn't have to be active in the moment of crisis to work. It just has to exist. Your body just has to know it's there.

Think of it this way. Stress is a weight. When you're carrying it alone, your body has to stay in high alert because there's no margin for error—if you stumble, if you drop it, no one's there to catch it or even notice it fell. When you have even one or two people who know what you're carrying, who've seen the weight and haven't walked away, the nervous system relaxes slightly. Not because they're literally holding the weight with you in some poetic shared-burden sense, but because the presence of backup changes the threat calculation your body is running in the background. Your body stops treating every stressor like a life-or-death emergency that you have to solve right now or die.

I saw this play out with a colleague a few years ago—someone I'll call Jamie because I'm not going to name them publicly, but the story is real and they know I tell it. Jamie was a high performer, the kind of person who made everything look easy, who you'd never worry about because they seemed to have it all together. Then their parent got sick. Cancer, the slow kind. Jamie was managing a full-time job, caregiving across state lines every other weekend, navigating insurance and hospice and the ten thousand small impossible decisions that come with watching someone die, and they told no one at work. Didn't ask for flexibility. Didn't mention it in meetings. Just kept showing up, getting quieter, getting thinner, the light going out behind their eyes in a way I noticed but didn't say anything about because I didn't want to pry.

Finally, they missed a major deadline. Completely forgot it existed. When their manager asked what was going on, Jamie broke down in the conference room. Told the whole story. Expected to get fired or at minimum put on a performance improvement plan.

Here's what happened instead. Their manager restructured their workload immediately. A few coworkers who'd been through similar situations reached out with specific, unglamorous advice—which hospice service to use, how to navigate the insurance labyrinth, what to say when the doctors start talking about "comfort measures." And Jamie's stress level didn't disappear. The parent still died three months later. But the quality of the stress changed. It went from drowning to treading water. Jamie started sleeping in longer stretches, three or four hours instead of ninety-minute fragments. Not because the situation improved—it didn't, not for months—but because they weren't holding it alone anymore. The weight was the same. The number of people carrying it had changed.

That's the thing about isolation most people don't understand until they've lived it. It doesn't just make stress harder to bear emotionally. It makes it *heavier* physiologically. Your body treats secrets like threats. When you're hiding what's really happening—even if you're hiding it to protect yourself, to avoid judgment, to stay professional, to not be "that person" who brings their problems to work—you're forcing your nervous system to maintain a constant low-grade alarm state. The act of *not* sharing, the energy it takes to perform normal when you're anything but, becomes its own separate stressor on top of whatever you're already dealing with.

You might be thinking, "Okay, but I don't have people I can talk to like that." Fair. Not everyone has a built-in support network, and telling someone who's isolated to "just connect" is about as useful as telling someone who's drowning to "just swim." If it were that easy, you'd already be doing it. I know that. I'm not going to pretend this is simple.

So let's break it down differently. Social support doesn't require a best friend or a therapist, though both help if you can access them. It requires *any* regular human interaction where you're not performing, where you can show up as you actually are—tired, frustrated, uncertain, half-broken—and not get punished for it.

For some people, that's a running group where nobody talks much but you're all moving together in the early morning cold, breath visible in the air, and there's something steadying about that shared quiet effort. For others, it's an online forum for people managing the same chronic condition, where you can say "I'm so tired of this" and get back a chorus of "same" from people who mean it. For others, it's one coworker who also thinks the company's new initiative is insane and you can vent to each other for five minutes in the breakroom without either of you trying to fix it or find the silver lining. The form doesn't matter. What matters is that your nervous system gets periodic evidence that you exist in relation to other people who see you, and that the performance mask can come off, even briefly.

Here's a real, well-documented case that stuck with me when I first read about it. After the 2011 earthquake and tsunami in Japan, researchers tracking cortisol levels in survivors found something they hadn't expected. The people who recovered fastest—physiologically, not just emotionally—weren't the ones who'd suffered the least damage or had the most resources or got the best temporary housing. They were the ones who'd maintained or quickly rebuilt social connections. Even in those awful temporary shelters, even grieving, even with everything they'd known wiped off the map, the survivors who were part of a community—cooking together, sharing stories, helping rebuild, just *being* together—showed faster normalization of cortisol rhythms than people who withdrew or ended up geographically isolated from others. The body registers connection as safety, even when the external circumstances are still objectively dire, even when there's nothing soft or comfortable about the situation.

Now, I'm not saying you need to survive a tsunami to understand this. The principle scales down. If your stress is chronic work pressure or financial strain or the slow grind of a relationship that's dying but not dead yet, the mechanism is the same. Isolation makes your body treat the threat as bigger and closer than it actually is. Connection recalibrates the threat level, gives your system a reference point that says *this is hard, but it's not kill-or-be-killed.*

But—and this is important, this is where people get it wrong and end up worse off than they started—not all social contact helps. Toxic relationships, interactions where you have to perform or defend yourself, environments where vulnerability gets weaponized or stored up as ammunition for later—those *increase* cortisol. You're better off alone than in a relationship that makes you feel less safe when you're in it. The support has to be genuine. It has to come from people who aren't trying to fix you, who aren't keeping score, who are just willing to witness that you're going through something hard without turning it into a referendum on your worth.

So how do you build that kind of connection when you're starting from scratch, when you've been isolated so long you've forgotten how to do this? You start small, and you start with proximity. You show up in the same place repeatedly. The gym at the same time each week. The same coffee shop on Saturday mornings. The same volunteer shift at the food bank. You're not trying to make best friends immediately. That's too much pressure and it shows. You're just letting your nervous system learn that there are people in the world who recognize you, who nod when you walk in, who'd notice if you stopped showing up. That low-level recognition—I see you, you see me, we're both here—is the foundation. It tells your body something it needs to hear: *You're not invisible. You're part of something, even if that something is small.*

From there, you look for the people who seem *real*. The ones who aren't performing, who'll admit when they're tired or frustrated, who don't need every interaction to be positive and uplifting and Instagram-ready. You don't have to share your life story in the first conversation. You don't have to trauma-dump on someone you barely know. You just have to be honest about small things. "Yeah, this week's been rough." That's it. You're testing whether honesty is punished or met with recognition. If it's met with recognition—"Same, I barely slept last night"—you've found someone whose nervous system is also tired of performing. That's the beginning of real connection, the kind that actually helps instead of just adding another layer of performance you have to maintain.

And here's the part that's hardest to accept, the part I still struggle with: you have to go first sometimes. You have to be the one who admits you're struggling, who asks if someone wants to grab coffee, who says out loud in a room of people who all seem fine that you're not okay. It feels vulnerable because it *is* vulnerable. It's exposing something true in a world that rewards the performance of having it together. But the alternative—waiting for someone else to reach out first, waiting until you feel less stressed before you try to connect, waiting for the perfect moment or the perfect person—keeps you in the loop indefinitely. Someone has to go first. It might as well be you.

I'll tell you what worked for me, after the dishes incident and the long stretch of terrible sleep that followed. I didn't overhaul my entire social life. I didn't join five groups or start seeing a therapist three times a week or move to a commune. I reached out to one friend I hadn't talked to in months, someone I knew had been through their own version of burnout, and I told them the truth. I was sleeping three hours a night. I was snapping at everyone. I didn't know how to stop. We didn't solve anything on that call. They mostly just said, "Yeah, that sounds fucking awful," and shared their own version of the dishes incident—theirs involved yelling at a grocery store clerk over a price difference of thirty cents. But afterward, that night, I slept for six hours straight. My body had been waiting for permission to stop treating everything as an emergency. Hearing someone else name the same struggle, knowing I wasn't the only one barely holding it together, gave my system that permission.

That's not a cure. It didn't fix the underlying work stress or the habits I'd built up over years of treating sleep as optional and isolation as strength. But it broke the loop long enough for my nervous system to downshift out of constant crisis mode, which gave me enough bandwidth to start addressing the other pieces—sleep hygiene, boundaries, the stuff we've talked about in earlier chapters. None of those tools work as well when you're trying to implement them while cortisol-drunk and alone, your system screaming that you don't have time to rest because there's no backup and if you stop moving you'll drown.

So here's what I want you to do, and I mean this as a literal next step, not a vague intention you'll think about later. Identify one person you could reach out to this week. Not to solve anything. Not to ask for advice or vent for an hour. Just to tell the truth about how you're actually doing. If you don't have that person yet—if you're starting from scratch or you've burned those bridges or you've been isolated so long you've lost the thread—identify one place you could show up repeatedly over the next month where you'd be around other people. A class. A group. A regular volunteer shift. Anything where you'd see the same faces more than once. You're not trying to make friends immediately. You're trying to give your nervous system evidence that isolation isn't your only option, that there are people in the world you could connect with if you decided to try.

And if you're thinking, "I don't have time for this, I'm barely holding it together as it is, adding another thing to my schedule will just make it worse"—that's the stress talking. That's the cortisol-fueled logic that says you have to do everything alone because asking for help or spending an hour with other people is a luxury you can't afford when there's so much to do. It's backward. The isolation is *why* you're barely holding it together. The time you spend connecting isn't time away from managing your stress. It's the thing that makes managing stress possible. It's the variable that changes whether you're trying to bail out a sinking boat alone or whether there's someone else in the boat with you, someone who can take the bucket when your arms give out.

Because here's what happens if you don't, if you keep running this program alone. The cycle tightens. Poor sleep feeds stress, stress feeds isolation, isolation feeds poor sleep. You start believing this is just how you are now—someone who doesn't sleep well, who's always on edge, who can't remember the last time they felt actually rested. You start thinking it's genetic or permanent or just the cost of being a functioning adult in the modern world. And your body keeps running the same program, night after night, because it has no new information to work with. It's still in survival mode. Still convinced the threat is close and backup isn't coming. Still waiting for a signal that never arrives.

Connection is the new information. It's the signal that shifts the program, the data point that tells your nervous system it's been miscalculating the danger. And the longer you wait to send that signal, the harder it gets to remember that another way of being is even possible, that there was ever a version of you who slept through the night and didn't startle awake at 3 a.m. with your heart pounding over nothing you can name.

The weight you're carrying doesn't have to get lighter for you to carry it differently. But you can't carry it alone forever and expect your body not to break under it.

Who's going to be in the boat with you?

My partner gave me the same look Darlene had given those fries weeks ago—not judgment, but recognition of someone caught in something they couldn't name. You've seen five ways the trap operates now. But none of those matter if you can't see it happening while you're in it.

Chapter 6: Chapter 6: Breaking the Cycle

The empty pint of Ben & Jerry's Half Baked sits on the counter next to the spoon. Both are evidence. Neither is memory.

11:47 PM. The exact same time I'd stood here with the almond butter jar three weeks ago. Different container, same trap, same margin of time when conscious decisions go dark.

Not one.

I stood here. Opened the carton. Must have tasted something—my mouth is sweet and there's that ice cream headache behind my left eye. But the experience itself? Gone. I was somewhere else entirely while my hand made the trip from container to mouth, solving a problem that didn't exist by creating one that does.

Three days ago I did the same thing with a bag of Hint of Lime Tostitos. Next week it'll be the Oreos in the cabinet behind the rice. The pattern doesn't care that I know better. That's the thing about stress eating most advice gets backward—not an information problem. You already know chips won't fix your deadline. Your body doesn't care what you know.

Seeing the trap isn't the same as escaping it. There's one exit that works faster than any other—and it's the one your stressed body insists you're too tired for.

Movement.

Not a workout. Not training for anything. Just the act of getting your body into motion when every signal you're receiving says to stay exactly where you are.

The research on this is unambiguous. A single ten-minute walk drops cortisol levels faster than any supplement, any breathing technique, any affirmation you can whisper to yourself in the bathroom mirror. Caroline worked with a trial group at Stanford—people with documented chronic stress, elevated cortisol markers, the works. Half were given cognitive behavioral therapy worksheets. The other half were told to walk for ten minutes whenever they felt the urge to stress eat.

The walking group's cortisol dropped an average of sixteen percent within twenty minutes. The worksheet group? No measurable change. Not because worksheets don't work—they do, for other things—but because you can't think your way out of a biochemical state. You have to change the chemistry first.

Your body interprets movement as evidence that the threat has passed. Sitting still is what prey does when the predator is close. Moving is what happens after you've escaped. Your nervous system doesn't know the difference between running from a bear and walking to the end of your driveway. All it knows is: muscles engaged, heart rate up slightly, we must be safe enough to move. Cortisol release slows. The signal to eat everything in sight fades.

This is why the advice to "just relax" fails so completely. Relaxation is a state you arrive at after safety has been established. Trying to relax while cortisol is flooding your system is like trying to fall asleep while someone's yelling in your ear. Your body will not permit it.

But movement? Movement your body understands as problem-solving. Not the imaginary problem of whether you're enough or whether you'll finish the project or whether anyone actually likes you. The immediate, physical problem of getting from here to there. Your brain is desperate for a problem it can actually solve. Give it one.

I learned this the hard way three winters ago. I was deep in a project deadline spiral—the kind where you wake up already behind and go to bed knowing you're further behind than when you woke up. I'd been eating standing up for two weeks. Actual meals at a table felt like time theft. My resting heart rate had climbed to seventy-nine, which doesn't sound dramatic until you know mine usually sits at fifty-eight.

A friend who'd watched me deteriorate suggested a walk. I told her I didn't have time for walks. She asked if I had time to keep eating pantry sleeves of crackers while refreshing my email. Fair point.

So I walked. Just to the corner and back, which in my neighborhood is maybe six minutes round trip. I didn't want to. Every step felt like time I should be spending fixing the thing that was broken. Except here's what happened: I got back to my desk and the thing I'd been stuck on for two days became immediately obvious. Not because walking gave me time to think about it—I specifically didn't think about it—but because moving my body for six minutes changed what my brain had access to.

The cortisol that had been holding my prefrontal cortex hostage let go just enough for me to see what I'd been staring past. I finished the stuck section in thirty minutes. Then I walked again. Then I worked again. I did this for three days straight and the project that had been eating me alive got done with a day to spare.

Was it the best work I've ever produced? No. But it was finished, coherent work instead of an abandoned disaster. And I didn't gain four pounds in the process, which had been my pattern with previous deadline crunches.

The pattern broke because I stopped trying to solve stress with stillness and started solving it with the thing my body was built for.

Here's what nobody tells you about exercise and stress: the benefits aren't cumulative in the way you'd expect. Going for a run on Sunday doesn't bank stress relief you can withdraw on Wednesday. But a ten-minute walk on Wednesday when you're about to eat the entire leftover pizza cold from the fridge works immediately. That's the part most advice gets backward. We're told to exercise regularly for long-term health, which is true and good and completely unhelpful when you're in the moment of deciding whether to demolish a pint of ice cream.

What helps in that moment is this: right now, before you open the freezer, walk to the mailbox.

You can still eat the ice cream after. Permission granted. You're not trying to willpower your way past the craving. You're just changing your biochemistry first, then deciding.

Most of the time, after the walk, the craving isn't gone but it's negotiable. It's no longer a scream. It's a suggestion. And suggestions you can talk to. Screams you can only obey or fight, and fighting costs energy you don't have.

This is why the trap is so effective. Cortisol creates the craving, the craving drives you toward the quick fix, the quick fix spikes your blood sugar, the crash twenty minutes later triggers more cortisol, and now you're in a tighter loop than where you started. The only exit is the thing that sounds least appealing when you're in it: getting up.

Not because getting up is virtuous. Not because you should want to. But because it's the biological interrupt that actually works.

There's a specific type of movement that works best, and it's not the type anyone's selling you. You don't need high-intensity anything. You don't need a gym membership or a Peloton or a program with a name. What you need is the thing researchers call "ambulatory activity sufficient to elevate heart rate ten to fifteen percent above resting for a minimum of eight minutes."

In human terms: a walk that makes you slightly aware of your heartbeat but doesn't leave you breathing hard.

That's it. That's the threshold where cortisol starts dropping. Go harder if you want—plenty of research supports vigorous exercise for stress reduction—but you don't need to. The trap releases at a much lower intensity than the fitness industry would have you believe.

I keep a pair of shoes by the door now for this exact reason. Not running shoes. Walking shoes. The kind I can slip on without unlacing. Because the moment between "I should move" and "I'm putting on shoes" is where the trap reasserts itself. If there's friction—if I have to find socks, tie laces, change clothes—my brain will generate seventeen reasons why later is better.

Later is never better. Later I'll be in a different part of the cycle, probably the part where I've already eaten the thing and now I'm dealing with the glucose crash on top of the original stress. The only moment that works is this one, and this one only works if the barrier to starting is as close to zero as possible.

Some people keep walking clothes in their car. Some change into them first thing in the morning and just stay in them until evening. Whatever removes one more decision point between stressed and moving.

The research team at UC San Diego tested this specifically. They gave one group detailed exercise plans—when to go, what route to take, how long to sustain what heart rate. The other group got one instruction: when you feel like eating something you know is stress-driven rather than hunger-driven, walk out your front door for ten minutes in any direction, then turn around and come back.

The detailed plan group exercised less frequently than the simple instruction group. Not because the plan was bad, but because a plan requires executive function, and executive function is precisely what cortisol impairs. The simple group just had to do one dumb thing: go outside, walk, come back. No decisions. No optimization. No wondering if they were doing it right.

Stress makes you stupid in specific ways. It doesn't rob you of intelligence—you can still solve complex problems, hold conversations, appear completely functional—but it murders your ability to start things that have multiple steps. This is why you can spend forty-five minutes scrolling your phone but can't seem to begin the work project that actually matters. The project has steps. The phone has none. Cortisol always picks the path with the fewest decision points.

So if you're designing an exit from the stress-eating trap, it has to be simpler than eating. Eating is: stand up, walk to kitchen, open thing, consume. Four steps, zero decisions. If your stress-relief strategy has more steps or more decisions than that, you'll default to food every time.

Walking out the front door for ten minutes is: stand up, put on shoes, go outside, move. Four steps. One decision, maybe two if you have to choose shoes. That's the threshold where it competes with food as the lower-friction option.

And here's the part that sounds too simple to work but does: it doesn't matter where you walk. It doesn't matter if you see anything interesting. It doesn't matter if you listen to music or a podcast or nothing. All that matters is that you move continuously for at least eight minutes.

The mechanism doesn't care about inspiration or scenery or optimal heart rate zones. It just cares that you shifted from stationary to ambulatory, and that you sustained it long enough for your endocrine system to register the change.

I've tested this in genuinely terrible conditions. Walking loops around a hospital parking garage at two in the morning during a family emergency. Walking up and down my hallway when it was too icy to go outside. Walking in place in a hotel room when I was too anxious to sit still but too self-conscious to leave. Every single time, the same result: the noise in my head got quieter, the urge to eat something crunchy and salty faded, and whatever I went back to afterward was manageable in a way it hadn't been eight minutes prior.

This isn't about becoming a person who loves exercise. You can hate every second of the walk. You can resent that you have to do it. What matters is that you do it anyway, because the chemistry doesn't care about your attitude. It only cares about the input.

For the first two weeks of trying this, I hated it. Every time I stood up to walk instead of opening the fridge, I felt like I was being punished for being stressed. Like I was adding one more task to an already impossible day. But I kept doing it because the alternative—continuing to gain weight while feeling progressively worse—was intolerable.

Somewhere around week three, something shifted. I stopped experiencing the walk as punishment and started experiencing it as the only ten minutes of my day where nothing was being asked of me. I wasn't solving problems or answering questions or trying to be someone I wasn't. I was just moving. That started to feel less like a burden and more like a shelter.

I'm not saying it became joyful. I'm saying it became neutral, which when you're trapped in a stress cycle is a massive upgrade.

The other thing that changed: I stopped gaining weight, then slowly started losing it. Not because I was burning massive calories on ten-minute walks—I wasn't—but because I was breaking the cortisol-craving-crash loop often enough that it lost its grip. I was still stress-eating sometimes, but not every day, not multiple times a day, not in the compulsive way where I'd look down and an entire bag of something would be gone without me tasting a single bite.

The weight loss was almost beside the point. What mattered more was that I got my evenings back. I stopped spending them in the foggy, restless state that follows a blood sugar crash. I could read again. I could have actual conversations instead of half-listening while mentally cataloging everything I should be doing instead.

People noticed. Not the weight—nobody mentioned that—but the fact that I seemed less frantic. A colleague asked if I'd started medication. I told her I'd started walking. She looked confused, like I'd answered a different question.

We've been taught to think of exercise as something you do for your body, separate from your mind. But that division doesn't exist in your biochemistry. When you move, you're not just burning calories or building muscle. You're directly altering the chemical environment your brain is operating in. Cortisol drops. Endorphins rise. Serotonin becomes more available. BDNF—brain-derived neurotrophic factor, the protein that helps neurons survive and grow—increases.

You're not running away from stress. You're running toward a different neurochemical state, one where the things that felt impossible ten minutes ago become just difficult. And difficult you can work with.

There's a specific window where this works best, and it's earlier than you think. Not after you've already eaten the entire box of crackers. Not after the stress has built to the point where you're immobilized. The moment to move is when you first notice the urge rising—when you catch yourself opening the pantry not because you're hungry but because you need to do something with your hands, your mouth, your restless trapped-animal energy.

That's the moment. Right there. That's when you need shoes on and body moving, because five minutes later the urge will have you, and once it has you the walk becomes exponentially harder to choose.

I started recognizing my tells. The way I'd drift toward the kitchen without deciding to. The way I'd open the fridge and just stand there looking, even though I'd looked thirty minutes ago and nothing had changed. The way my jaw would clench and unclench like I was chewing something that wasn't there.

Those became my cues. Not to fight the urge—fighting it just made it louder—but to redirect it. To take the energy that was reaching for food and aim it at the door instead.

Some days this worked smoothly. Other days it was a fight every single step. There were days I'd get halfway down the block and turn around, convinced I was wasting time I didn't have. Then I'd get back and immediately want to eat something, and I'd realize I'd just made it worse by starting and stopping.

The pattern that emerged: if I could get to eight minutes, the urge would fade. If I stopped before eight minutes, it would come back stronger. Eight minutes appears to be the minimum dose. Not because of anything mystical about that number, but because that's roughly how long it takes for the cortisol curve to start dropping in response to movement.

Less than eight minutes and you're in the weird middle zone where you've activated your cardiovascular system but haven't sustained it long enough to shift your endocrine response. You've paid the cost of starting without getting the benefit of completion. That's the zone where it's easy to decide the whole thing is pointless.

Which is why I started setting a timer. Not to push myself to go longer—though sometimes I would—but to give myself permission to stop at ten minutes and know I'd done enough. Because the trap wants you to believe that unless you're doing it perfectly, doing it hard, doing it long enough to really count, you might as well not bother.

Ten minutes counts. Eight minutes counts. Six minutes is better than zero, though it might not be enough to break the cortisol loop. But ten minutes, every single time, is enough.

I've done this enough now that I can feel the shift happen. It's not dramatic. There's no moment of clarity or burst of energy. It's more like pressure releasing. The static in my head doesn't go away, but it gets quieter. The thing I was avoiding doesn't become appealing, but it stops being impossible.

And that's all you need. Not motivation. Not inspiration. Just the shift from impossible to possible. From there you can actually function.

The hardest part isn't the movement itself. It's overriding the voice that insists you don't have time, you're too tired, it won't help anyway, you'll do it later, you need food first, you need to finish this one thing first, you need to deserve it first.

That voice is cortisol talking. It sounds like you. It uses your reasoning style, your vocabulary, your exact patterns of self-justification. But it's not you. It's your stress response trying to keep you in the same state you're already in, because to your nervous system, the known threat is safer than the unknown solution.

This is the same mechanism that keeps people in bad relationships, bad jobs, bad cities. Not because they don't know better, but because the familiar bad thing feels safer than the unfamiliar potentially good thing. Your body will pick the devil it knows every single time unless you consciously override it.

And overriding it doesn't mean convincing yourself you want to walk. It means walking anyway while the voice is still talking. The voice doesn't stop. You just stop waiting for it to give you permission.

After a few weeks of this, something else started happening. I'd be in the middle of work, not particularly stressed, and I'd feel the urge to walk. Not to escape anything. Just because my body had learned that moving for ten minutes made everything after it easier. It started requesting it the way it requests water when you're thirsty.

That's when I knew the pattern had actually changed. Not because I'd become someone who loves exercise—I still don't, particularly—but because my body had updated its database of what solves problems. Food was no longer the only entry. Movement was in there too, and increasingly it was the first option my system reached for instead of the last resort.

This didn't happen through willpower. It happened through repetition. Through choosing the walk enough times that my nervous system started to trust it as a viable option. Through proving, over and over, that ten minutes of movement would reliably deliver the relief that food promised but never actually provided.

Now when I feel the pull toward the kitchen and I know I'm not hungry, I don't have to fight it. I just think: shoes, door, ten minutes. And most of the time, that's enough to get me moving. Not because I'm disciplined. Because the path of least resistance changed.

That's the thing about breaking the cycle. You're not trying to become a different person. You're trying to give your current person a better option, then choose it enough times that it becomes automatic.

The cycle breaks when the new pattern becomes easier than the old one. Not more virtuous. Not more impressive. Just easier. And it becomes easier through repetition, not revelation.

You will not wake up one day suddenly free of the urge to stress eat. But you might wake up one day and realize you haven't done it in three days, then a week, then longer. Not because the urge disappeared, but because you caught it earlier each time and redirected it before it had you.

That's what breaking the cycle actually looks like. Not dramatic transformation. Just earlier intervention, repeated until it's routine.

Chapter 7: Chapter 7: Physical Activity

You've told yourself you're too tired to exercise. Maybe for six months. Maybe longer. And maybe that's true—you are tired. But tired is what the trap feels like from the inside, and 'too tired to move' is how the trap keeps you there.

Here's what actually happened during those six months.

The less I moved, the worse I felt. The worse I felt, the more I reached for foods that would spike my blood sugar and crash it two hours later. Every crash made the couch more magnetic. Made the idea of movement more impossible. I'd watch people jogging past my window and feel something between envy and contempt—*must be nice to have that kind of energy*—as if energy were something you either had or didn't, not something your own choices were actively destroying.

This isn't a chapter about getting in shape. It's not about fitness goals or workout plans or finally becoming the person who owns running shoes that aren't gathering dust in the closet. It's about understanding that your body processes stress through movement, and when you stop moving, you're essentially asking your nervous system to handle a crisis with one hand tied behind its back.

Let me tell you about some baboons in Kenya.

In 1994, Robert Sapolsky—a neuroendocrinologist who'd spent years studying stress in the wild—was observing a troop of baboons in the Serengeti. He wasn't studying exercise, exactly. He was studying what happens to bodies under chronic social stress. Baboons have brutal hierarchies. The lower you rank, the more abuse you take. Constant vigilance. Random attacks from higher-ranking males. Food insecurity. Sound familiar?

What Sapolsky found was predictable: the low-ranking baboons had chronically elevated cortisol. Their bodies were marinating in stress hormones all day, every day. No surprise there.

But here's what wasn't predictable.

The baboons who engaged in regular, vigorous physical activity—chasing, climbing, wrestling, even just ranging across long distances to forage—showed significantly lower baseline cortisol levels even when their social stress remained constant. They weren't less stressed in terms of what they faced. They were just processing it differently. The activity didn't eliminate the stressor. It changed how their bodies metabolized it.

Your body is running the same firmware those baboons were running. When stress hits, cortisol floods your system to mobilize energy. It's preparing you to fight or flee. To run from the predator or fight off the threat. But if you never actually fight or flee—if you just sit at your desk or your couch while your heart rate climbs and your blood sugar spikes—that cortisol has nowhere to go. It just circulates, looking for something to do. And eventually it starts breaking things down. Muscle tissue. Bone density. Your ability to sleep through the night. Your willingness to eat a reasonable dinner instead of half a sleeve of cookies standing in front of the open pantry at nine-thirty at night. (I'm still working on this one, by the way. Some weeks are better than others.)

Movement completes the stress cycle. It gives your body the physical follow-through it's expecting. The thing it was preparing you to do.

I'm not talking about punishing yourself on a treadmill or suffering through a boot camp class where someone screams at you about your lack of commitment. I'm talking about the thing your body is already wired to do in response to stress—the thing we've culturally trained ourselves to ignore in favor of "powering through."

The woman who helped me understand this wasn't a fitness expert. She was a health psychologist named Kelly McGonigal, and for years she'd been teaching stress management at Stanford the way most of us understand it: stress is bad, you need to reduce it, here are some breathing exercises and mindfulness techniques. Standard stuff. Then she started looking at the research more closely—actually reading the studies instead of just accepting the cultural narrative—and she realized something uncomfortable.

The data didn't actually show that stress itself was the problem.

The problem was stress *plus inactivity*.

The people who reported high stress but also engaged in regular physical activity didn't show the same negative health outcomes as the people who reported high stress and were sedentary. Same stress levels. Different bodies. The difference wasn't how much stress they faced or how well they managed their thoughts about it. It was whether they moved.

McGonigal started running experiments. She'd bring people into the lab, stress them out with impossible tasks and social rejection scenarios—the kind of thing that sends cortisol through the roof—and then measure what happened next. The people who went for a twenty-minute walk immediately afterward saw their cortisol drop back to baseline within an hour. The people who sat quietly in a waiting room, resting and recovering the way we're all told to do, stayed elevated for three hours or more.

Three hours of cortisol bathing your system, telling your body you're still in danger, you still need to mobilize energy, you still need to be ready to run. Except you're not running. You're sitting. And your body is very, very confused about what to do with all that mobilized energy.

So it stores it. Usually as fat. Often around your midsection, because that's where your body likes to keep emergency fuel close to your vital organs.

This is the part where I'm supposed to tell you to start exercising. To get up right now and go for a walk or download a fitness app or join a gym. But you already know that exercise is good for you. Everyone knows that. If knowing were enough, you'd already be doing it. The question isn't whether movement helps. The question is why it's so goddamn hard to actually do the thing when you're already stressed and tired.

Here's the answer nobody wants to hear.

Because stress makes you stupid.

Not permanently. Not in every domain of your life. But in the moment, when cortisol is high, your brain literally shifts resources away from the prefrontal cortex—the part that plans, decides, weighs long-term consequences—and toward the amygdala, the part that screams DANGER, FIND COMFORT NOW. This is why you can know, intellectually, that going for a walk would make you feel better, and still find yourself face-down in a bag of chips at three in the afternoon. Your thinking brain knows the walk is the answer. But your stress brain is in the driver's seat, and it's not interested in long-term solutions. It wants immediate relief. And food delivers that faster than movement. Food is right there. Movement requires you to stand up, change clothes, leave the house, exert effort. When your amygdala is running the show, that equation doesn't even register as a choice.

So if you're waiting until you feel motivated to exercise, you're waiting for the wrong signal. Motivation is a luxury your stress brain doesn't traffic in.

What works is smaller than motivation. It's decision-making that happens *before* the stress brain takes over.

There's a concept in behavioral psychology called implementation intentions. It's just a fancy way of saying: decide the specific when and where ahead of time, so you don't have to decide in the moment. "I will exercise" is a goal. "I will walk around the block at 12:15 p.m., right after I finish my lunch" is an implementation intention. The first one requires motivation and willpower and the right mood and enough energy. The second one just requires a clock.

This is what actually worked for me—not inspiration, not a new workout program, not finally getting my life together after years of telling myself I would. I started putting my shoes by the door the night before. That's it. The whole system. I didn't commit to running five miles or doing a YouTube workout or going to the gym. I committed to putting on my shoes and standing outside for sixty seconds.

Sixty seconds. You can do anything for sixty seconds, even when you feel like death.

Most days, once I was outside, I'd walk. The barrier was gone. The hardest part was already done. Some days I'd just stand there, feel the air on my face, notice the temperature, and go back inside. But the threshold was so low that my stress brain couldn't build a convincing argument against it. It couldn't muster the energy to fight me on sixty seconds.

After two weeks, I noticed I was sleeping better. After a month, I noticed I wasn't reaching for my usual 3 p.m. snack with the same desperation. I still wanted it—I'm not pretending I became some zen monk who doesn't crave sugar—but it wasn't the same frantic, white-knuckle need. It was just... a want. And wants are easier to negotiate with than needs.

I can't tell you it fixed everything. I still have terrible days where I don't move at all and I eat my feelings and I go to bed disgusted with myself. I still have to trick myself into going outside more often than I'd like to admit. But the baseline shifted. The engine light isn't on constantly anymore. And that makes everything else—the food choices, the sleep, the mood, the ability to handle a bad day without completely falling apart—that much more possible.

Now let me tell you about Sarah.

Sarah is a marketing director at a mid-sized tech company. Two kids under eight. A husband who travels for work three weeks out of the month. When I met her, she was eating cereal for dinner three nights a week. Not because she loved cereal or because it was some kind of nostalgic comfort food. Because by the time the kids were in bed—homework done, teeth brushed, the fourteen small battles of bedtime finally won—the idea of making a real meal felt like climbing a mountain. And cereal was right there. In the cupboard. Requiring zero effort. And her stress brain said *yes, that, now*.

She knew she needed to move more. Everyone told her that. Her doctor told her that at her annual physical while looking at her blood pressure numbers with concern. Her mother told her that in the gentle, worried way mothers do. She told herself that every time she saw a photo of herself and didn't recognize the exhausted person looking back. But every time she thought about actually fitting in a workout, her brain would start running the math.

Get up earlier? Already exhausted, already waking up at 5:30 to get the kids ready for school.

Exercise during lunch? That's the only time she had to actually eat something and maybe answer emails without someone interrupting her.

Work out after the kids go to bed? That was the only time she had to herself, the only hour of the day that wasn't about managing someone else's needs.

None of it added up. So she just... didn't. And felt guilty about it. And ate more cereal.

What changed wasn't her schedule. Her schedule was exactly as impossible after as it was before. What changed was the size of the ask.

She started taking the stairs at work instead of the elevator. Four flights, twice a day. Once in the morning when she arrived, once after lunch. That was it. Not a workout. Not even exercise, really, in the way we usually think about exercise. Just stairs. Just choosing the slower, harder route between two floors.

She did that for three weeks and noticed that her afternoon energy crash—the one that usually hit around 2 p.m. and left her useless until she could mainline coffee or sugar—wasn't hitting as hard. So she added a ten-minute walk during her lunch break. Not to get steps. Not to burn calories or optimize her fitness or achieve some goal. Just to get outside and move her body through space. To remember that she had a body, that it could do things, that the world existed outside the four walls of her office.

Two months in, she noticed something strange.

She wasn't eating cereal for dinner anymore. She was making actual food. Not elaborate meals—not the kind of thing you'd post on Instagram or serve to guests—but real food that required more than opening a box. Scrambled eggs. A salad. Leftovers from the weekend. Sometimes just toast and cheese and some cut-up vegetables. But it was food she'd chosen and prepared, not food she'd grabbed because her brain was too tired to do anything else.

She didn't white-knuckle her way out of the cereal habit. She didn't make a rule or set a goal or join a program. She just stopped wanting it. Or rather, she started having enough bandwidth to want something more than just the easiest possible option.

What happened in her body is the same thing that happened in McGonigal's lab, the same thing that happened to those baboons in Kenya. The physical activity completed the stress cycle. Her cortisol was still spiking during the day—the deadlines didn't go away, the kids didn't become easier, her husband didn't stop traveling—but it wasn't *staying* elevated for hours. It was moving through her system and clearing out, the way it's supposed to. The way it was designed to. And when cortisol isn't running the show, your prefrontal cortex comes back online. You start making decisions that align with what you actually want, not just what your stress brain is screaming for in the moment.

Sarah didn't transform into a marathon runner or a fitness influencer. She still doesn't love exercise. She still has weeks where she doesn't take the stairs because she's too tired or too rushed or just doesn't feel like it. But she walks most days. Takes the stairs most days. Does a fifteen-minute yoga video on weekend mornings if the kids sleep in. It's not impressive. It's not Instagram-worthy. It won't win her any awards or admiration. But it's consistent. And consistency is the only thing that changes your baseline cortisol.

Here's the part that trips people up, the part where the fitness industry has sold us a story that's actively counterproductive:

Exercise doesn't have to be hard to work.

We've internalized this idea that if you're not sweating, if you're not breathless, if you're not sore the next day, then it doesn't count. That's gym culture talking. That's the fitness industrial complex trying to sell you programs and supplements and the idea that you need to suffer to earn results. It's not physiology.

The research on cortisol and movement shows that moderate-intensity activity—walking, easy cycling, swimming, gentle yoga—produces the same cortisol-lowering effect as high-intensity interval training. Same effect. Different experience. The difference is that moderate activity doesn't spike cortisol first. High-intensity exercise actually raises cortisol in the short term, because you're stressing your body. You're creating a crisis. And then, yes, it drops afterward. For most people, that's fine. Their baseline is low enough that they can handle the spike and still come out ahead.

But if you're already running high on stress—if your baseline cortisol is elevated because of work or relationships or money or the general state of the world—adding more acute stress to your system can backfire.

I learned this the hard way, and I'm still a little bitter about the time I wasted.

There was a year where I convinced myself that if I was going to exercise, it needed to be brutal. It needed to hurt. I'd do these high-intensity interval workouts—twenty minutes of burpees and sprints and jumping lunges, the kind of thing that leaves you in a heap on the floor, gasping, muscles screaming. And I felt virtuous afterward. I felt like I'd conquered something. Like I'd proven something to myself about discipline and toughness.

But I also felt hungry all the time. Ravenous. The kind of hunger where you eat a full meal and you're still looking around the kitchen thirty minutes later trying to figure out what else you can eat. And I was exhausted. Not the good kind of tired where you sleep well and wake up refreshed. The kind where you're tired all day and then can't fall asleep at night because your nervous system is wired.

My sleep got worse. My mood got worse. I wasn't losing weight—I was gaining it, even though I was "working out" more than I ever had. And I couldn't understand why the thing that was supposed to fix my stress was making everything worse.

Turns out, I was just jacking up my cortisol even higher. I was taking a system that was already maxed out and demanding more from it. And my body was responding the only way it could: by demanding more fuel and more rest. I wasn't breaking the stress cycle. I was amplifying it.

When I finally switched to walking—just walking, nothing fancy, no speed goals or distance targets—the cravings dropped. My sleep improved. I lost the weight I'd been trying to lose with the brutal workouts. Not because I was burning more calories. I wasn't. But because my body wasn't in constant crisis mode anymore. It wasn't desperately trying to store every calorie against the next emergency.

This is the thing about cortisol that nobody tells you, the thing that makes all the standard fitness advice miss the point: it doesn't care about your intentions. It doesn't care whether you're stressing your body with work deadlines or with a workout you read about in a magazine or saw on TikTok. Stress is stress. A crisis is a crisis. And if you're already maxed out, more stress—even the "good" kind, even the kind you're choosing—isn't the answer.

What your body needs when it's already running on fumes is movement that signals safety.

Long, easy walks. Stretching. Dancing in your kitchen to a song you love. Swimming. Anything rhythmic, repetitive, and not too hard. Anything that says to your nervous system: *we're okay, there's no emergency here, you can stand down.*

The technical term for this is rhythmic bilateral movement, and it's one of the most effective ways to regulate your nervous system. When you walk, your left foot and right foot alternate in a steady rhythm. When you swim, your arms alternate. When you dance, your whole body moves in rhythm with the music. This bilateral stimulation—this back-and-forth, left-right pattern—has a calming effect on the amygdala, the part of your brain that's screaming about danger and demanding immediate relief.

It's the same mechanism that underlies EMDR therapy for trauma. Therapists use bilateral eye movements or tapping to help people process traumatic memories without getting overwhelmed. The rhythm tells your brain: we're safe. We're in our body. We're here, now, and nothing is chasing us.

And when your brain gets that message, when it actually believes it, your cortisol follows. It stands down. It stops mobilizing energy for a crisis that isn't happening.

This is why a twenty-minute walk can do more for your stress levels than an hour of scrolling your phone on the couch, even though the couch feels easier in the moment. The couch doesn't complete the stress cycle. It just pauses it. It distracts you. And when you get up, when the distraction ends, the cortisol is still there, waiting. The crisis is still happening in your body even if your mind has temporarily checked out.

Let me tell you about something that happened last Tuesday, because this is still my life, I'm still working on this, I'm not standing here as someone who has it all figured out.

I had a terrible morning. Back-to-back meetings that went long. A project I'd been working on for weeks imploded because of a decision made by someone three levels above me who'd never even looked at what we were building. An email thread that spiraled into conflict—the kind where everyone is being professionally polite but you can feel the hostility radiating through the screen. By noon I was furious and exhausted and wanted nothing more than to go home, close the blinds, order takeout, and eat my feelings in front of Netflix.

Instead, I went for a walk.

Not because I'm disciplined or virtuous or because I've transcended my stress-eating patterns. Because I've done this enough times now that I know—really know, in my body, not just in my head—what happens if I don't. I know that if I go home and eat my feelings, I'll feel better for about twenty minutes and then I'll feel worse. And the worse will last the rest of the day and probably into the next morning.

So I walked. For thirty minutes. Didn't solve anything. Didn't have any grand insights or breakthrough moments. Didn't even really think that much. Just walked, looked at trees, noticed the temperature of the air, let my feet hit the pavement in that steady left-right rhythm.

When I got back, I wasn't furious anymore.

I was still tired. Still frustrated with the project, still annoyed at the email thread, still dealing with all the same problems. But I wasn't in crisis mode. The engine light had turned off. I made a reasonable lunch—not a perfect lunch, not a meal I'd post on Instagram, but real food that I ate sitting down instead of standing over the sink. I answered emails without snapping at anyone. I got through the rest of the day without imploding.

That's all I'm asking your body to do. Not to become an athlete. Not to transform into someone who loves exercise or runs marathons or posts workout selfies. Just to complete the cycle so you're not carrying the wreckage of every stressor around with you all day, letting it pile up until the weight of it crushes you into making choices you don't actually want to make.

Now, here's the practical problem, and this is where most advice falls apart:

You already know this. Everyone knows that exercise helps with stress. Everyone knows that movement is good for you. The gap isn't knowledge. It's implementation. And most implementation advice is garbage because it assumes you have more bandwidth than you actually do. It assumes you're starting from a place of stability and just need a little push in the right direction.

But you're not starting from stability. You're starting from depletion. And the advice that works for someone with a full tank doesn't work when you're running on fumes.

So let's talk about what actually works when you're already exhausted.

First: it has to be so easy that you can't talk yourself out of it.

If your plan is "I'll go to the gym three times a week," you've already lost. Your stress brain will find twelve reasons why today isn't the day. Too tired. Too busy. Didn't sleep well. Have too much work. Don't have the right clothes. The gym will still be there tomorrow. But if your plan is "I'll walk to the end of the block," that's harder to argue with. You can do that in the clothes you're already wearing. You can do that tired. You can do that upset. You can do that in two minutes.

Second: it has to happen at the same time every day.

This is the implementation intention thing I mentioned earlier. Your brain likes routines because they don't require decisions, and decisions are expensive when you're stressed. Every decision costs you something. Every time you have to weigh options and choose, you're spending bandwidth you don't have. But if you walk at the same time every day, it stops being a choice. It stops being something you have to decide. It just becomes what you do at that time.

I walk at 7 a.m. Every day. Not because I'm a morning person—I'm absolutely not, I hate mornings, I would sleep until nine every day if I could—but because if I wait until later, the day eats me alive and it never happens. Something always comes up. Work calls. Emails. Errands. The plan to walk at lunch becomes the plan to walk after work becomes the plan to walk tomorrow. But at 7 a.m., nothing has happened yet. The day hasn't started making demands. It's just me and my shoes and the door.

Third: it has to be something you don't hate.

This sounds obvious, but people ignore it constantly. They force themselves to run because running burns the most calories, even though they despise running. They join boot camp classes because everyone says high-intensity is the most efficient, even though they spend the entire class wishing it would end. And then they wonder why they can't stick with it. Why they keep quitting. Why the motivation never lasts.

If you hate running, don't run. Walk. Bike. Swim. Dance in your living room. Garden. Play with your dog. Chase your kids around the backyard. The best exercise is the one you'll actually do. And you won't do something you hate unless someone is paying you or yelling at you or you're trying to prove something that isn't worth proving.

Fourth: it doesn't have to be long.

Fifteen minutes is enough to lower cortisol. Ten minutes is better than nothing. Five minutes is better than zero. You're not training for a marathon. You're not trying to win a fitness competition or impress anyone. You're completing a stress cycle. That's a low bar. You can meet it.

Here's what this looked like for me when I first started, when I was still in the phase of telling myself I was too tired:

I put my shoes by the door every night. Right by the door, where I'd trip over them in the morning. In the morning, I'd put them on—just putting them on, that was the whole commitment—and then I'd walk outside and stand there for sixty seconds. That was it. That was the entire promise I made to myself.

Most days, I'd end up walking around the block. Because once I was outside, once I'd cleared the threshold of the door, the barrier was gone. The hard part was done. But on the days I didn't walk, on the days I really did just stand there for sixty seconds and come back in, I still counted it as a win. Because I'd kept the promise. I'd put on the shoes. I'd gone outside. And keeping the promise is what builds the habit, not the number of steps or the minutes logged or the calories burned.

After a month of this, I extended the promise to five minutes. After two months, ten minutes. After six months, I was walking thirty to forty minutes most mornings. Not because I'd set some ambitious goal or made a New Year's resolution or finally gotten serious about fitness. But because it felt worse to skip it. My body started to expect it. It became part of how I woke up, part of the morning routine, like brushing my teeth or making coffee.

And the cravings—this is the part that still surprises me, even though I know the biology, even though I've read the studies—just... softened.

I still want sugar sometimes. I still stress-eat occasionally. I still have days where I eat half a bag of chips without really noticing until the bag is empty. But it's not the same desperation. It's not the white-knuckle, need-this-now, can't-think-about-anything-else feeling that used to hit me every afternoon like clockwork. My cortisol is lower. My sleep is better. My baseline mood is steadier. And all of that makes it easier to make reasonable choices about food, because I'm not constantly operating from a state of emergency.

Here's the thing nobody tells you about building a movement habit when you're stressed, the thing that causes most people to quit right before it would have worked:

The first two weeks are a lie.

You won't feel better. You might feel worse, because you're adding one more thing to your day and your body hasn't adjusted yet. You're tired, and now you're making yourself move when you don't want to, and it feels like punishment, and you don't understand why everyone says this is supposed to help because you feel terrible.

This is where most people quit. They think, "Exercise is supposed to make me feel better, and I feel terrible, so clearly this isn't working for me. My body must be different. This advice must not apply to me."

But you're not supposed to feel better in week one. You're not broken. Your body isn't different. You're just in the adjustment phase, the phase where you're asking your system to do something new before it understands why.

The payoff comes later. Around week three, when you notice you slept through the night without waking up at 3 a.m. with your mind racing. Week four, when you realize you didn't have your usual afternoon crash. Week six, when you notice you made dinner instead of ordering takeout, and you didn't even think about it, it just happened.

The benefits are cumulative. They're not immediate. They're not dramatic. You won't wake up one morning transformed. But you'll wake up one morning and realize that the thing that would have destroyed you last month is just... a hard day. You got through it. You didn't fall apart.

And if you're looking for immediate relief, if you quit before you get to the good part, you'll never know what you missed.

Sarah told me that around week five, she almost stopped. She was tired of taking the stairs. They weren't feeling any easier. Her legs still hurt. She was still out of breath by the fourth floor. And she didn't see the point. Nothing had changed. She didn't feel different. She didn't look different. What was the point of doing something hard if it wasn't making anything better?

But she kept going. Not because she was disciplined or motivated. Because she'd told a friend she was doing it, and she didn't want to admit she'd quit. That's it. That's the only reason. Pure stubbornness and not wanting to look like a quitter.

And then, in week six, she had a brutal day at work.

Everything went wrong. A product launch she'd been managing for months fell apart at the last minute because of a vendor screw-up. Her boss was furious, even though it wasn't her fault. She missed her son's soccer game because of a last-minute emergency meeting that didn't actually solve anything. She got home at eight-thirty, fully expecting to collapse. To cry. To order pizza and eat half of it standing in the kitchen while her kids asked her questions she didn't have the energy to answer.

But she didn't collapse.

She made dinner. Not a fancy dinner, just spaghetti and jarred sauce and a bag of frozen vegetables, but she made it. She helped with homework. She read her daughter a bedtime story. She even laughed at something her son said, really laughed, the kind that comes from somewhere genuine and not just polite parenting.

And she realized, later that night when she finally sat down: a month ago, a day like that would have destroyed her. She would have been in tears. Rage-eating crackers. Snapping at her kids for asking normal kid questions. Lying awake until midnight replaying every moment and hating herself.

But this time, she got through it. Not because the day was less hard. Because her baseline resilience was higher.

That's what movement does. It doesn't eliminate stress. It doesn't make bad days stop happening or protect you from things going wrong. It raises the threshold for what breaks you. It gives you a little more room between the stressor and the collapse. And in that room, you can make different choices.

There's a researcher at Harvard Medical School named John Ratey who wrote a book called *Spark*, and the whole premise is that exercise is the single most effective thing you can do for your brain. Not your body—your brain. Not your cardiovascular health or your muscle mass or your waistline. Your actual brain, the organ that's supposed to be running the show.

He shows data on how regular movement increases something called BDNF—brain-derived neurotrophic factor—which is essentially fertilizer for your neurons. It helps them grow, form new connections, repair damage. It improves memory. Focus. Mood regulation. Stress resilience. The people who exercise regularly don't just have lower cortisol in the moment. They have more *capacity* to handle cortisol when it spikes. Their brains are physically better equipped to process stress without breaking down.

They're not less stressed. They're more resilient. And resilience is the thing that makes the difference between reaching for the chips or reaching for an apple. Between spiraling after a bad day or just getting through it. Between feeling like your life is out of control or feeling like you can handle what's in front of you.

This isn't about willpower. It's not about being strong or disciplined or finally getting your act together. It's about biology. When your brain is working properly—when it's getting the movement and the neurochemical support it needs—you make better decisions without trying. The decisions just feel easier. The good choice stops feeling like deprivation and starts feeling like the thing you actually want.

Here's the last thing I want to say about this, because it's the part that people get wrong and then give up entirely, the part where the fitness industry has done real damage:

Exercise is not a punishment for eating.

It's not something you do to earn food or to atone for last night's pizza or to burn off the calories from the cookie you ate this morning. If that's your framework—if you're using movement as penance—you've already lost. Because you're just reinforcing the same shame cycle that's driving the stress eating in the first place. You're telling your body it's bad, it needs to be punished, it can't be trusted. And your body responds to that message the same way it responds to any threat: by trying to protect you. By holding onto resources. By craving more.

Movement is a gift you give your nervous system. It's a signal that says: *I'm taking care of you. I see that you're overwhelmed. I'm going to help you complete this stress cycle so you don't have to carry it around all day.*

When I finally understood that—when I stopped thinking of exercise as something I had to do and started thinking of it as something I got to do, something that made my life easier instead of harder—everything shifted.

I stopped forcing myself to do workouts I hated. Stopped punishing myself with extra miles when I ate too much. Stopped using my watch to track every step and calorie and minute like they were evidence in some case I was building against myself. I just moved because it felt better than not moving. Because my body worked better when I did. Because the version of me who walks is calmer, sleeps better, makes better choices, and doesn't spend every afternoon white-knuckling her way past the vending machine.

And here's what nobody tells you, what you can't know until you've lived it for a while: eventually, the movement starts to feel like the easy part. The part you don't have to think about. And the choices that used to feel impossible—passing up the donut, going to bed instead of scrolling for another hour, not eating the entire bag of chips just because you opened it—those start to feel possible.

Not because you've become a different person. Because your body is finally working with you instead of against you.

Movement gets you out in the moment. But cortisol has been rewriting your metabolism for weeks or months, and those changes don't reverse the day you start moving again.

Chapter 8: Chapter 8: Food for Thought

Cortisol changes what your body does with food. Not what you crave—that's a different mechanism—but what happens after you swallow: where the calories go, how your cells respond to insulin, which tissues get fed and which stay locked out. You can eat the same meal at the same time two days in a row, and cortisol will route the calories to completely different places.

The three prescriptions had been sitting in my medicine cabinet for two months—sleep, metabolism, digestion—before I understood they were all treating the same thing.

I tell you this not because I figured it out on my own (I didn't), but because the moment she said it, I could trace the whole mess back to one source: I was eating like someone trying to put out a fire with gasoline.

Before I explain how to fix this, I need you to understand what it costs you to keep doing it.

Picture this: It's 3 PM on a Tuesday. You've been in meetings since nine, you skipped lunch or grabbed something fast, and now you're staring at your screen with that specific kind of exhaustion that feels like your brain is wrapped in cotton. You can't think clearly. You can't focus. You reach for something—anything—that will get you through the next two hours. A candy bar from the vending machine. A large sweetened coffee. Maybe both.

For about twenty minutes, you feel better. Alert. Almost human again.

Then the crash hits. Harder than before. You're irritable now, foggy, and somehow hungrier than you were an hour ago. So you eat something else. Maybe you tell yourself you'll have a light dinner to compensate, but by the time you get home you're so drained that cooking feels impossible, so you order takeout or heat up something fast and heavy. You eat it in front of the TV because you're too tired to do anything else. You go to bed feeling full but not satisfied, and you sleep badly, and you wake up already tired, and the whole cycle starts again.

Now stretch that pattern across weeks. Months. Years.

Your clothes don't fit the way they used to, but you're eating *less* than you did five years ago, or at least it feels that way, so what's wrong with you? You're tired all the time but you can't sleep through the night. Your stomach hurts more days than not. You get sick more often. You're shorter with people you care about. You can't remember the last time you felt genuinely rested or genuinely happy about anything.

And here's the part that really gets you: you blame yourself. You think it's a discipline problem. A character flaw. If you just had more willpower, more control, you could eat better, sleep better, feel better. The fact that you can't must mean something is fundamentally wrong with you.

It doesn't. What it means is that you're stuck in a biochemical feedback loop that's designed to tighten every time you try to fight it with willpower alone. And until you understand the mechanism, you're going to keep losing that fight.

Here's what's actually happening.

Cortisol is supposed to be your body's emergency response system. Something threatening happens—a predator, a near-miss car accident, a genuine crisis—and cortisol floods your bloodstream, jacks up your blood sugar, sharpens your focus, gets you ready to fight or run. Then, when the threat passes, cortisol levels drop back down and your body returns to normal. That's the design. That's how it's supposed to work.

But chronic stress—the kind that comes from work deadlines, financial pressure, relationship tension, the general background hum of modern life—keeps cortisol elevated. Your body can't tell the difference between a real physical threat and the anxiety you feel checking your email at 11 PM. So cortisol stays high. And one of the things high cortisol does, reliably and ruthlessly, is hijack your relationship with food.

Elevated cortisol increases your appetite, particularly for high-sugar, high-fat foods. Not because you're weak or undisciplined, but because your body thinks you're in a famine or fleeing danger, so it wants calorie-dense fuel to survive whatever crisis it believes you're facing. At the same time, cortisol tells your body to store fat, especially around your midsection, because visceral fat is metabolically active and quick to mobilize in an emergency. And it interferes with insulin function, which means your blood sugar regulation goes haywire. You get hungrier faster, crash harder, crave sweets more intensely.

Now here's where the trap clicks shut: the foods you reach for when you're stressed—the cookies, the chips, the fast food, the sugary coffee drinks—cause your blood sugar to spike and then plummet, which your body reads as *more stress*, which triggers *more cortisol*, which makes you crave *more junk food*. It's a trap with a ratchet mechanism. Every turn tightens it. Every attempt to white-knuckle your way through it just makes you hungrier and more stressed.

I'm not talking about occasional indulgence. I'm talking about the pattern where stress makes you eat poorly, which makes the stress worse, which makes you eat even more poorly, until you're stuck in a loop that feels impossible to break. And the whole time, you're blaming yourself for lacking willpower, when the real problem is that you're fighting your own biochemistry without realizing it.

Let me give you an example that isn't me.

Oprah Winfrey has talked publicly, many times, about her lifelong struggle with weight and emotional eating. In one interview, she described how stress from work would send her straight to the kitchen, looking for comfort in mashed potatoes or bread—foods that gave her a temporary sense of calm but left her feeling worse an hour later. She's one of the most successful, disciplined, driven people on the planet. She's built an empire. She's influenced millions of people. And even she has wrestled with this pattern for decades.

That should tell you something. This isn't about willpower. This isn't about being weak or lazy or lacking discipline. It's about understanding the mechanism and working *with* your body instead of against it.

Or look at Dwayne Johnson. The man is famous for his discipline, his work ethic, his physical transformation from football player to action star. And yet he's been open about the fact that he has regular "cheat days" where he eats massive amounts of comfort food—pancakes, pizza, sushi, brownies—because the psychological and physiological pressure of maintaining that level of discipline all the time is unsustainable without a release valve. Even someone with that much discipline and support (personal trainers, meal prep services, a clear financial incentive to stay in shape) can't just power through cravings indefinitely.

So if you're sitting there thinking, "Yeah, but I should be able to just eat better," I need you to stop. That's not how this works. You're not failing. The strategy is failing.

So what does working with your body actually look like?

Start with what *not* to do, because I think that's more useful than another list of superfoods you're supposed to eat.

Don't try to overhaul your entire diet overnight. Don't go on a restrictive cleanse or cut out entire food groups or start skipping meals to "reset" your system. I've tried all of those. They work for about a week, maybe two, and then the deprivation itself becomes a stressor, cortisol spikes again, and you end up bingeing on the exact foods you swore off. The cycle just gets tighter. The shame gets heavier. You're worse off than when you started.

What *does* work—slowly, unglamorously, but reliably—is making small, specific swaps that stabilize your blood sugar and don't feel like punishment.

Here's what I mean. Let's say you're used to grabbing a muffin and coffee for breakfast. That's refined flour and sugar, which spikes your blood sugar fast and then drops it just as fast, leaving you irritable and hungry by 10 AM. Instead, try oatmeal with a handful of walnuts and some berries. The oats are complex carbs—slower to digest, steadier energy. The walnuts add healthy fat and protein, which slows digestion even more. The berries give you a bit of sweetness without the crash. It's not a dramatic change in terms of effort or time. You're still eating breakfast. You're still getting something warm and satisfying. But the effect on your blood sugar—and your cortisol—is significant.

Or let's say you're in the habit of reaching for chips or candy in the afternoon when your energy tanks. Swap that for an apple with almond butter, or carrot sticks with hummus, or a small handful of almonds. You're still getting something to eat. You're still satisfying the urge to crunch or chew. But you're giving your body nutrients that actually support stable energy instead of spiking and crashing it.

I know how this sounds. It sounds like the advice you've heard a thousand times: eat more fruits and vegetables, choose whole grains, blah blah blah. And you're thinking, "Yeah, I *know* that, but when I'm stressed out of my mind at 9 PM, I'm not reaching for baby carrots."

I get it. I've been there. I've stood in front of an open fridge at 10 PM, exhausted and wired at the same time, knowing that what I *should* do is go to bed and that what I'm *about to* do is eat half a pint of ice cream standing up in the kitchen. The gap between knowing what's good for you and actually doing it can feel enormous when you're stressed. Knowing doesn't close the gap. Understanding the mechanism doesn't automatically change your behavior. You still have to make the choice, in that moment, when you're tired and stressed and you just want something that makes you feel better right now.

So let me reframe this, because I think the usual advice misses something important: the goal isn't to eliminate comfort eating. The goal is to understand *why* you're eating and choose foods that actually comfort you instead of just numbing you temporarily.

When you're stressed and you eat something sugary or fatty, what happens in your brain is this: you get a brief dopamine hit—pleasure, relief, a moment where the noise in your head quiets down. Then, within an hour or two, you crash. The relief evaporates. You feel sluggish, guilty, maybe a little sick. Your stress is still there, but now it's accompanied by physical discomfort and a layer of shame about what you just ate. It feels like comfort in the moment, but it's not. It's a chemical bait-and-switch.

Real comfort—the kind that actually reduces cortisol—comes from foods that support serotonin production, reduce inflammation, and stabilize your mood over time. And a lot of those foods are genuinely delicious, once you start paying attention to how they make you feel an hour or two after eating them instead of just in the first three bites.

For example: dark chocolate—like, 70% cacao or higher—contains compounds that can lower cortisol and improve mood. A couple of squares after dinner genuinely helps, and it doesn't spike your blood sugar the way milk chocolate does. You're still getting the ritual of eating something sweet at the end of the day. You're just choosing a version that works with your body instead of against it.

Fatty fish like salmon or mackerel are loaded with omega-3 fatty acids, which reduce inflammation and have been shown in multiple studies to improve mood and reduce anxiety. I started eating salmon once or twice a week, and I noticed—not immediately, but over a few weeks—that I felt more stable. Less reactive. Not transformed, but steadier.

Leafy greens like spinach are high in magnesium, which helps regulate cortisol and supports your nervous system. Nuts, seeds, whole grains—all of these things actively calm your stress response instead of aggravating it.

And here's the part that surprised me: once I started eating more of these foods consistently, my cravings for junk actually decreased. Not because I was white-knuckling my way through temptation, but because my body wasn't on the blood-sugar rollercoaster anymore. When your energy is stable, you don't get those desperate 3 PM cravings that feel like life-or-death hunger. You just feel... steady. It's not dramatic. It doesn't feel like a revelation in the moment. But it's sustainable. And sustainability is what actually matters here, because a diet you can only stick to for two weeks isn't a solution.

Let me tell you about magnesium specifically, because this one changed things for me and I think it flies under the radar.

Magnesium is involved in over 300 biochemical reactions in your body, including the regulation of cortisol. When you're stressed, your body burns through magnesium faster than usual, which means chronic stress often leads to magnesium deficiency, which then makes you *more* reactive to stress. Another feedback loop. Another way the trap tightens.

Foods high in magnesium include almonds, cashews, spinach, black beans, avocado, dark chocolate (there it is again), and whole grains like quinoa and brown rice. I started adding a handful of almonds to my breakfast and making sure I had spinach or another leafy green with lunch. Within a couple of weeks I noticed I was sleeping better and feeling less on-edge during the day. Not cured, not transformed—but noticeably better. Less likely to snap at someone in traffic. Less likely to spiral into anxiety at night.

Small shifts. Real effects.

Now, you might be thinking: "Okay, but what about when I'm genuinely hungry and stressed and I just want something that tastes good and makes me feel better *right now*?"

Fair question. And here's the thing: you don't have to choose between food that supports your cortisol levels and food that actually tastes good. The two aren't mutually exclusive. You just have to expand your definition of what comfort food can be.

Take gut health, for example. There's been a lot of research over the past decade showing that the bacteria in your gut—your microbiome—communicate directly with your brain via the vagus nerve. It's called the gut-brain axis, and it's not metaphorical. It's a literal biochemical communication network. When your gut is healthy, it produces neurotransmitters like serotonin (about 90% of your body's serotonin is made in your gut, not your brain) and GABA, which regulate mood and reduce anxiety. When your gut is inflamed or out of balance—from a diet high in sugar and processed foods, from chronic stress, from antibiotics—that communication breaks down, and you end up more anxious, more reactive, more prone to stress.

Foods that support a healthy gut microbiome include fermented foods like yogurt, kefir, sauerkraut, kimchi, and miso. Fiber-rich foods—fruits, vegetables, whole grains, legumes—feed the good bacteria. And here's the part that matters for taste: a lot of these foods are genuinely flavorful and satisfying once you get used to them. Greek yogurt with berries and a drizzle of honey is delicious. Kimchi on rice or in a stir-fry is incredible—spicy, tangy, complex. Miso soup is savory and comforting in a way that feels almost meditative.

The shift isn't from "foods I like" to "foods I'm supposed to eat." It's from foods that give you a short-term dopamine spike and then make you feel worse, to foods that genuinely nourish you and improve how you feel over time. That's the reframe. That's the thing that makes this sustainable instead of just another diet you start and abandon.

But let's be honest: this isn't a one-and-done fix. I still mess this up regularly. Last week I had a stressful deadline and I ate an entire bag of tortilla chips for dinner. Not with salsa. Not with guacamole. Just chips. Standing in the kitchen. At 9 PM. Did it help? No. Did I feel great about it afterward? Also no. Did I do it anyway because in that moment I was too fried to care? Yes.

The point isn't perfection. The point is recognizing the pattern, understanding what's driving it, and making different choices *more often than not.* If you can shift your baseline from mostly junk food to mostly whole foods—even if you still have those nights where you eat chips for dinner—you're breaking the cortisol trap. You're giving your body the nutrients it needs to handle stress without spiraling.

One more thing that matters here: *when* you eat, not just *what* you eat.

Eating large, heavy meals late at night interferes with sleep, but it also keeps your cortisol elevated because your body is working hard to digest food when it's supposed to be winding down. I used to eat dinner at 9 or 10 PM, sometimes later, because I was working late and then finally stopping to eat when I was already exhausted. My sleep was terrible. My digestion was terrible. Everything felt harder than it should have.

Now I try to eat dinner by 7 PM, and if I'm hungry later I'll have something light—a piece of fruit, a small handful of nuts, maybe some yogurt. That's it. It's a small change, but it made a noticeable difference in how I feel in the morning. I wake up less groggy, less bloated, more ready to handle the day. Not every morning. Not perfectly. But enough that I keep doing it.

Hydration, too. This is so obvious it almost feels silly to mention, but: if you're dehydrated, your body interprets that as a stressor, which raises cortisol. And a lot of us walk around mildly dehydrated all day without realizing it, because we're drinking coffee or soda or nothing at all instead of water. I keep a water bottle on my desk now and make myself finish it twice during the workday. That's it. That's the whole strategy. But it helps. My head is clearer. My energy is steadier. I'm less likely to reach for sugar when I'm actually just thirsty.

Here's another thing nobody talks about: the ritual of eating matters almost as much as what you eat.

When you eat standing up in the kitchen, or in your car, or at your desk while answering emails, your body stays in stress mode. You're not relaxing. You're not digesting properly. You're just shoveling food in while your nervous system is still revved up from whatever you were just doing.

Contrast that with sitting down at a table, even if it's just for ten minutes. Putting your phone away. Actually tasting what you're eating. That shift—from eating as a task you're trying to get through to eating as a moment where you pause—makes a physiological difference. Your parasympathetic nervous system kicks in. Your digestion improves. You feel more satisfied with less food because you're actually present for the experience.

I'm not saying you have to light candles and play soft music every time you eat. I'm saying: sit down. Put the phone away. Taste your food. That's it. It sounds minor, but it's not.

So here's what I want you to take from this, not as a lecture but as something I'm still figuring out myself:

Food isn't just fuel. It's information you're giving your body about whether it's safe or under threat, whether it's nourished or depleted, whether it should ramp up the stress response or dial it down. When you eat foods that spike your blood sugar, increase inflammation, and deplete key nutrients, you're telling your body, "We're in crisis mode. Stay alert. Store fat. Stay hungry." When you eat foods that stabilize your blood sugar, support your gut, and provide the nutrients your body actually needs, you're telling it, "We're okay. You can relax."

That doesn't mean you have to eat perfectly all the time. It means you have to eat *intentionally* most of the time, with an understanding of what you're doing and why.

Start small. Pick one meal—breakfast, probably, because it sets the tone for the rest of the day—and make it a meal that stabilizes your blood sugar instead of spiking it. Oatmeal with nuts and fruit. Eggs with vegetables and whole-grain toast. Greek yogurt with berries and seeds. Something that gives you protein, healthy fat, and fiber instead of just sugar and refined carbs.

Do that for a week. Notice how you feel. Notice what happens to your energy mid-morning. Notice whether you're reaching for snacks as desperately as you usually do.

Then add another change. Maybe it's swapping your afternoon snack. Maybe it's eating dinner earlier. Maybe it's just drinking more water. Maybe it's sitting down to eat instead of standing at the counter.

You're not trying to overhaul your entire life overnight. You're trying to give your body a little more of what it needs and a little less of what's making the stress worse. That's it. That's the whole strategy.

Because here's the thing: you can't think your way out of a cortisol problem, and you can't willpower your way out of it either. But you can eat your way toward better management of it, one meal at a time, one choice at a time, until the pattern shifts and the trap loosens its grip.

And once you've got your food dialed in—even imperfectly, even most of the time instead of all of the time—the next piece falls into place a lot easier. Which brings us to sleep. Because if you're eating in a way that supports your cortisol levels but you're still only getting five hours of broken sleep a night, you're trying to bail out a sinking boat with a teaspoon. Sleep is where all of this either consolidates into real progress or unravels back into the same old patterns.

The three prescriptions had been sitting in my medicine cabinet for two months—sleep, metabolism, digestion—before I understood they were all treating the same thing. You've seen the trap's architecture now: how it operates, how to recognize it, how to exit it. The question left is how to build a life where you don't fall back in.

Chapter 9: Chapter 9: Moving Forward

I watched the notification pop up on my phone at 11:47 PM. A former client—Sarah, who'd hired me three years ago to help her lose the thirty pounds that appeared during her startup's Series B funding round—had just posted on LinkedIn about pulling her fourth all-nighter this month.

I stared at that post for probably five full minutes, drafting and deleting various responses. What I wanted to write: *Your adrenal glands don't care about your funding round. They just know you've been forcing them to operate in crisis mode for so long they've stopped knowing what normal feels like.*

I didn't post it. Partly because Instagram-lecture-comments help nobody, but mostly because I'd have been a hypocrite. Two years ago I would've been in those comments cheering her on, probably adding my own humble-brag about the eighty-hour week I'd just survived. The cortisol flooding my system wasn't a warning signal—it was my résumé, proof I was important enough to be needed.

Here's what finishing a book like this doesn't give you: immunity from your own material. I still catch myself treating stress like a credential that needs constant renewal. Last Tuesday I snapped at my partner for "interrupting my flow" when all he did was ask if I'd eaten anything since breakfast. It was 4 PM. I genuinely couldn't remember whether I'd had lunch. Twenty minutes later I found myself standing in front of the open refrigerator eating cold pad thai directly from the container with my hands, wondering why I felt so spacey and irritable.

My body doesn't care that I was on deadline. It doesn't accept "just finishing this chapter" as a valid reason to ignore its signals. It just knows I overrode the hunger cues for six hours, my blood sugar crashed, my cortisol spiked to compensate, and now my executive function has gone offline and I'm making terrible food decisions while standing on cold tile in my socks.

That's the thing about the cortisol system—and I know I've been saying "that's the thing about" too much in my own writing lately, it's become a verbal tic I'm trying to break—it doesn't negotiate with your justifications. You can tell yourself the stress is temporary. That you'll rest after this project ships, after you get through this week, after you finally prove yourself enough times that the anxiety will magically evaporate. Your adrenal glands aren't participating in that conversation. They're just responding to the signals: threat detected, flood the system, prepare for crisis. They were designed to do this for ten minutes while you outran a predator, not for ten months while you white-knuckle your way through an understaffed department and a culture that mistakes exhaustion for dedication.

You've spent eight chapters learning the mechanics. How chronic stress rewires ghrelin and leptin, turning your hunger signals into a scrambled radio station you can't quite tune in. How poor sleep compounds cortisol elevation, which tanks your insulin sensitivity, which makes everything worse. How isolation amplifies the stress response and movement dampens it. How the bag of chips at 9 PM was never about willpower—it was about a blood sugar crash meeting elevated cortisol meeting a brain that's been running on fumes for so long it'll grab any fast fuel it can reach.

Knowing all of this doesn't automatically translate into doing differently, though. Does it?

I think about James Clear writing *Atomic Habits* after spending years rebuilding his life following the baseball injury that fractured his skull in high school. He didn't write that book from the mountaintop, looking down at the masses who hadn't figured out habit formation yet. You can feel the scar tissue in every chapter. The systems he describes aren't theoretical—they're the ones he actually used, including all the parts where he backslid and had to start over. The book landed with millions of people because it wasn't a lecture. It was a trail map from someone who'd actually walked it, including the sections where he'd slipped backward down the hill.

That's where you are right now. Not at some finish line—there isn't one—but at the trailhead where you've learned enough to recognize the path. You can see the stress patterns forming before they fully take over. You can feel the difference between actual physical hunger and the anxiety-driven urge to eat *something, anything* to quiet the noise in your head. You've probably had at least one night where you implemented the sleep routine from Chapter 4 and woke up genuinely rested for the first time in months, shocked at how different your brain felt when it wasn't operating through fog.

You've probably also had nights where you said "screw it" and stayed up until 2 AM scrolling through other people's curated highlight reels on Instagram, then spent the next day moving through molasses, forgetting why you walked into rooms.

Both of those experiences are data. The second one isn't failure.

This is usually where books like this give you the numbered action plan. Five steps to maintain momentum. Three keys to lasting transformation. A tidy framework you can screenshot and tape to your bathroom mirror.

I'm not going to do that. Those lists imply there's a formula, and there isn't. What exists instead is a continuous practice of paying attention to what your body is actually communicating, rather than what your stress-soaked brain insists is urgent.

Let me tell you about Michael Pollan's seven-word framework: "Eat food. Not too much. Mostly plants." It's possibly the most-quoted nutrition advice of the last twenty years. People love it because it's simple. But if you actually read *In Defense of Food*—the book that line comes from—you realize the simplicity is hard-won. Pollan spent two hundred pages dismantling nutritionism, the industrial food system, the whiplash of conflicting dietary science, the cultural anxiety around eating. *Then* he gives you those seven words. The simplicity isn't reductive. It's clarifying. It's what remains when you strip away all the noise and pressure and marketing.

The cortisol version might be: *Notice the signal. Respond before it escalates. Build a life that doesn't require constant override.*

Sounds simple. Try actually doing it in a culture that actively rewards the override.

The culture celebrates the person who works through lunch. Who answers emails at 11 PM. Who shows up to the meeting while sick because "the team is counting on me." We've constructed an entire economy on people ignoring their bodies' stress signals long enough to develop the chronic diseases we then sell them medications and solutions for. You're trying to step out of that cycle, which makes you an outlier.

Outliers get friction.

Your coworker who brags about her seventy-hour weeks will, consciously or not, try to pull you back in. Not because she's malicious—because your boundary forces her to look at her own lack of one. When you leave at 5:30 to make it to your cycling class, her staying until 8 PM stops being virtuous and starts being a choice she has to examine. That's uncomfortable. Easier to make a comment about "must be nice to have that kind of flexibility" and let the implication hang there.

Your family might not understand why you're "suddenly so rigid" about sleep schedules or meal timing or needing an uninterrupted hour to yourself on Sunday mornings. The culture around you is still treating stress as proof of importance. You're trying to treat it as the warning light it actually is.

This is where everything from the previous chapters stops being interesting intellectual content and starts being lived friction.

Take the sleep piece from Chapter 4. You understand now that cortisol follows a circadian rhythm—peaks in the morning to wake you up, drops at night so you can sleep. Chronic stress flattens that curve. You wake up exhausted. You're wired at 11 PM. The fix makes perfect sense on paper: consistent sleep and wake times, a real wind-down routine, no screens in the bedroom, maybe some magnesium glycinate an hour before bed.

In practice? It means saying no to the late-night work email from your boss in Tokyo. It means disappointing your friend who wants to text-vent at midnight about her relationship. It means sitting with the discomfort of *not* numbing out with Netflix when your brain is absolutely screaming that you should be doing something productive, anything productive, because rest hasn't been earned yet.

I still screw this up constantly—and there I go again, interrupting my own teaching to acknowledge I haven't mastered this, which is exactly the tendency I mentioned in my author notes but it's genuinely true. I'll have a week of solid sleep, feel absolutely incredible, then convince myself I can "just this once" stay up late to finish something, and within forty-eight hours my entire system is destabilized again. The 3 PM sugar crash. The irritability. The standing-in-front-of-the-fridge-eating-with-my-hands thing. It all comes roaring back fast.

What's different now: I notice it faster. I know what actually works to restabilize. I'm not spiraling for three weeks anymore. I'm spiraling for three days, maybe four, then catching it.

That's progress. Not the Instagram version. The real version.

Same with the eating patterns from Chapter 8. You've learned that cortisol dysregulates ghrelin and leptin, the hormones that signal hunger and fullness. You've practiced eating slowly, actually tasting your food, identifying emotional hunger versus physical hunger. Maybe you've had meals where it genuinely worked—where you ate until you were satisfied, not stuffed, and didn't think about food again for four hours.

Maybe you've also had days where you white-knuckled through the morning, told yourself you were "too busy" to eat a real lunch, then annihilated an entire box of Wheat Thins at 4 PM while standing in the pantry, barely registering the taste.

The question isn't whether you'll have those days. You will. The question is what happens next.

The old pattern—the one this entire book has been working to dismantle—treats the Wheat Thins incident as moral failure. Proof you're undisciplined. Evidence you'll never get this right. The shame spiral kicks in, cortisol spikes further, and you're off to the races.

The new pattern recognizes it as a predictable physiological response to skipping lunch while under stress. Your blood sugar crashed. Your cortisol surged to compensate by mobilizing stored glucose. Your brain, desperate for fast energy, overrode your rational decision-making and went straight for simple carbs. That's not a character flaw. That's your endocrine system doing exactly what it evolved to do when you ignore it long enough.

Once you see it as a system response instead of a personal failing, you can intervene at the actual leverage point. Not the crackers. The missed lunch.

What got in the way of feeding yourself at a reasonable time? Was it actually that you were too busy, or that you've internalized the message that taking a lunch break is somehow indulgent? Was it that you didn't have easy food available, which points to a planning gap? Was it that you were so deep in stress-mode you didn't even register hunger until it became a crisis?

Different root causes require different fixes. All of them require paying attention to your actual experience instead of what you think should be happening.

Brené Brown makes a distinction in *Daring Greatly* that's relevant here: the difference between shame and guilt. Guilt says "I did something bad." Shame says "I am bad." Guilt can be generative—it points you toward repair, toward doing differently next time. Shame just makes you want to hide, which for most of us means more stress, more cortisol, more dysregulated eating, more standing in front of the fridge at 9 PM wondering how we got here again.

The work is catching the shame story before it takes over. Noticing when you're about to spiral into "I'm so undisciplined, I'll never figure this out," and redirecting to "Okay, what was the actual sequence of events? Where can I intervene differently next time?"

It sounds straightforward. It's not easy, especially if you've spent years—maybe decades—treating your body like an obstacle to overcome rather than a system to work with.

That's the real shift this book is asking you to make. Not just learning strategies. Fundamentally changing your relationship to your own physiology. Stopping the constant override. Actually listening to the signals instead of treating them like inconvenient noise that gets in the way of your real priorities.

This means you're going to disappoint people. You're going to set boundaries that feel uncomfortable. You're going to choose rest over productivity sometimes, even when every socialized instinct screams that rest must be earned and you haven't done enough yet to deserve it.

You might lose the respect of people who measure worth in busyness. You'll probably confuse family members who don't understand why you're "making such a big deal" about things that seem minor to them—why you can't just stay up late this once, why you need to eat at regular times, why you're being so "rigid" about protecting your morning routine. You will definitely face moments where the old pattern—push through, override, prove yourself—feels easier than the new one.

The old pattern has a cost, though. You know that now. Not just intellectually, but in your body. You've felt the difference between a week where you slept enough, ate regularly, moved, connected with people who actually see you—and a week where you didn't. The contrast is undeniable once you've experienced both sides.

So what are you willing to protect?

Not in some theoretical future when everything calms down and you have more time. That future doesn't exist. Right now. This week. Today.

What's one thing you can do in the next two hours that signals to your body it's safe to come out of crisis mode? Maybe it's eating lunch at an actual table instead of in front of your screen. Maybe it's a fifteen-minute walk outside, no phone, no podcast, just walking. Maybe it's texting the friend who makes you laugh instead of the one who needs something from you.

It doesn't have to be big. It just has to be real.

Then tomorrow, you do it again. Not because you're following a protocol, but because you're building a life where the stress response is the exception rather than the baseline you've learned to tolerate.

That's what the other side of this looks like. Not perfect adherence. Not never slipping up. Just a slow, unglamorous shift in what you're willing to accept as normal.

Your body has been trying to tell you something for a long time. Maybe years. The signal started quiet—a little fatigue here, some weight around your middle that wasn't there before, trouble falling asleep. You learned to ignore it because there was always something more urgent demanding your attention. That's what functional adults do, right? We push through.

The signal got louder. You got better at ignoring it.

But the push-through stops working eventually. The cortisol doesn't just spike and settle anymore. It stays elevated. The weight doesn't come off with a few good weeks. The sleep doesn't improve on its own. Your body stops whispering and starts shouting, and suddenly you're dealing with fasting blood sugar in the pre-diabetic range, blood pressure numbers that make your doctor frown, anxiety that won't quit no matter how much you try to logic your way out of it, a metabolism that feels like it's shut down entirely.

That's not failure. That's what happens when a system designed for short-term crisis gets forced into long-term deployment.

You're here because you're ready to listen. Not to another diet plan. Not to another productivity framework. To the actual signal your body has been sending.

So listen.

Notice what it feels like when you're adequately rested versus running on five hours of sleep and caffeine. Notice the difference between eating because you're actually hungry versus eating to manage anxiety or boredom or the vague feeling that something is missing. Notice how your body feels after you move versus after you sit for six hours straight. Notice which people in your life leave you feeling energized and which ones leave you feeling drained.

You already know most of this. You've known it for a while, probably. The question is whether you're willing to act on what you know, even when it's inconvenient. Even when it costs you the approval of people who are still stuck in the override pattern. Even when it means admitting that you can't actually do it all, be everything to everyone, maintain the pace you've been running.

The body doesn't care about your deadlines or your reputation or how many people are counting on you. It just knows whether it's in crisis mode or not.

Make it safe.

Not someday when things calm down. Now. Today. With the next decision in front of you—the one about whether you'll eat lunch or power through, whether you'll go to bed at a reasonable hour or scroll for another forty minutes, whether you'll say yes to one more obligation or finally say no.

Your body is still signaling. The question is whether you're finally ready to respond.

Also in the Series

Every book in Weight Loss Reset stands on its own — read them in any order. If this one was useful, the library continues:

The Stuck Point

The Long Way Down

The Midlife Reset

Off the Rules

Off the Cycle

The Comfort Trap

The Stall

The Last Diet

Eating in the Dark

www.ingramcontent.com/pod-product-compliance
Lightning Source LLC
LaVergne TN
LVHW010730061126
851857LV00014B/1419